Published by Siduri Books 2010

2 4 6 8 10 9 7 5 3 1

First published in Great Britain in 2010 by
Siduri Books
3 Quarry Villas, Wells Road
Easton, Somerset BA5 1EE
UK

www.siduri.co.uk

A CIP catalogue record for this book is available from the British Library

ISBN 978-0-9562052-1-6

Printed by
TJ International Ltd
Padstow, Cornwall, UK

the mechanics of songwriting:
a guitarist's guide

leo coulter

with illustrations by
laura howell

Siduri books

contents

about this book

THE TERMINOLOGY NEEDED TO explain the inner workings of music is so specialised that it is considered the preserve of musicians who have been through years of formal musical training. In opposition to this idea stands *The Mechanics of Songwriting*, which aims to reveal these inner workings to guitarists of all musical backgrounds and levels of musical education.

The Mechanics of Songwriting is the only book in the English language that has been written with this aim. It should not be confused with books that offer general advice on songwriting or books that provide an introduction to music theory, although it does introduce elements of music theory and it does explore the songwriting process. *The Mechanics of Songwriting* is different because it is bolder; it wants songwriters to possess the full complement of ideas through which alone a broad, career-altering understanding of songs and songwriting can be reached.

So you should bear in mind that you have been betrayed by your government, you're low on ammo and no one expects you to make it out of this alive. In other words, you will need to absorb a number of unfamiliar and sometimes onerous ideas in quick succession if you are to attain the new understanding of music's inner workings you have been promised. There is no escaping the fact that the ease with which the following opening chapters can be read has been compromised by

this bold ambition, and it is unavoidable that at times you will need to read *The Mechanics of Songwriting* slowly, meticulously, and with a guitar in hand. Above all, you will need to have faith that the many new ideas and definitions you are encountering have not been included in the book for their own sake, but are vital to the book's aim.

The good news is that every effort has been made to mitigate the difficulties inherent to *The Mechanics of Songwriting*'s subject matter. The book has been conceived and written in such a way as to invite re-reading, for example, and care has been taken to introduce new technicalities with concise, crystalline language that forbids misinterpretation. Interviews with renowned songwriters illuminate adjacent technical chapters, while musical examples tend to involve well-known, guitar-friendly songs that can be found easily online. Availing yourself of a digital music service such as Spotify should grant you access to recordings of most if not all of the songs to which this book refers.

chapter one: chords - a crash course

what is a chord?

A CHORD IS A GROUP of two or more notes played simultaneously. If you play any two notes anywhere on the guitar, that's a chord. The tricky question is not, 'What is a chord?', it's 'What are the criteria by which a chord is named?'. You can probably play an A major chord, but you might not understand why that particular selection of notes is called an A major chord.

All major and minor chords are triads. A triad is a chord consisting of three notes, each one separated from its neighbour by the interval of a 3rd. Whoa there, time for another question in big letters...

what is an interval?

An interval describes the distance between two notes. The smallest interval you will encounter is called a minor 2nd. If you play two adjacent notes on the guitar – by holding down fret 3 (C) followed by fret 4 (D♭) on the A string, for example – you will hear the interval of a minor 2nd. If you play the same initial note (C) followed by an open G string, you will hear the interval of a perfect 5th.

It is important that you acquire some understanding of intervals before you attempt to understand the constitution of a chord. However, it is also important that this examination of chords is not interrupted by extended digressions, particularly for the sake of those readers already familiar with intervals. For this reason, an explanation of intervals and how to calculate them can be found on pages 42-45.

what is a chord? (take two)

It's worth repeating that all major and minor chords are triads. Let's build a C major chord by figuring out the three notes that comprise the chord: root, third and fifth.

The first note is easy, it's the root note of C major: C. To get our next note, known as the third of the triad, we need to add the note that is the interval of a major 3rd above the root note. Finally we need to find the fifth of the triad, which is a perfect 5th above the root note, or a minor 3rd above the previous note (the third) if you prefer. For the purpose of finding out which notes are a major 3rd and a perfect 5th above C, we can simply use a C major scale (see page 186). The third and fifth notes in this scale are a major 3rd and a perfect 5th above C respectively. So the three notes in a C major chord are: C (the root), E (the third) and G (the fifth). Whenever you play these three notes at the same time you are playing the chord of C major.

Cmaj

> ### *If there are only three notes in a major chord, why am I usually playing at least four strings?*
>
> *It often feels as though you are playing more than three notes when you play a major chord on the guitar. In a sense there are often more than three notes because the root, third or fifth might appear more than once in a chord shape. The familiar open E major chord shape is a good example.*
>
> **Emaj**
>
> *The root, third and fifth in an E major chord are E, G# and B. Ordered from thick E string to thin E string, the notes in the E major shape above are E, B, E, G#, B and E. In musician-speak, we could say that the fifth of the chord, B, is 'doubled at the octave'; the B on the second fret of the A string is doubled by the B of the open B string an octave higher. Similarly, there are three Es in the chord shape, each an octave higher than the last. Spend a few minutes analysing some of the major chord shapes in your vocabulary, working out which notes are the root and which the third and fifth of the triad.*

minor chords

Minor chords are just like major chords; triads consisting of root, third and fifth. The crucial difference is the interval between root note and third, which is a minor 3rd rather than a major 3rd. Or to put it another way, a C major and a C minor chord share the same root and fifth, while the third is slightly different. The third in a minor chord is one semitone lower than the third in a major chord.

Major and minor chords get their name from the type of third above the root.

● *Can I use a scale to figure out the notes of a chord?*

Yes, so long as the scale you use has the same name as the chord you're trying to build. For example, you would need to use the scale of B minor to figure out a Bmin chord. Scale degrees I, III and V equate to the root, third and fifth of the corresponding chord.

---

semitones and tones

These are terms used to describe the two smallest intervals, the minor 2nd and the major 2nd. By moving from fret one to fret two on a guitar string you are moving up by one semitone. If you move from fret one to fret three on a guitar string (or from fret five to fret seven, or eleven to thirteen, for example) you are moving up by a tone. Whenever you are moving 'stepwise' from one note to another – as in a major scale – you are moving in intervals of semitones or tones. For the sake of clarity, people sometimes refer to tones as 'whole tones'.

Let's use our open Emaj and Emin chord shapes as an example.

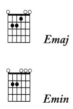

Emaj

Emin

The root, third and fifth in an E major chord are E, G♯ and B, as we have already seen. An E minor chord should have the same root and fifth (E and B) as an E major chord, and a third that is one semitone below the third in an E major chord. So G♯ becomes G♮.

In the same way, we can turn a C major chord into a C minor chord by changing the third of the chord from E to E♭.

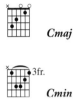

There are, of course, chords that are not simply called major or minor. There are fifth chords, diminished chords, seventh chords and so on, chords that consist of four, five or six notes rather than just three. But before we look at chords in more detail, we should examine a chronically misunderstood concept among guitarists, that of key.

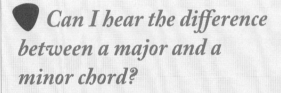

introducing key

If you are going to write a piece of music, whether it's a simple pop song or a full requiem mass, it is absolutely essential that you understand key. Unfortunately, most guitarists – even most guitar teachers – do not fully understand functional harmony. The phrase 'functional harmony' refers to the way chords and notes function and interact within the context of a key.

Just a moment ago we asked the question, 'What are the criteria by which a chord is named?' You may now have a better understanding of how a chord is constructed; you may even be able to build your own major and minor chord shapes using this knowledge. But what really defines a chord, what gives a chord meaning within a piece of music, is its relationship with the chords around it and the key of the music.

so what is key?

The first thing to understand about key is that every passage or piece of music has a note that is called the tonic note. The tonic note is the note the music seems to be gravitating towards, a note that sounds more final than the other notes in the passage or piece. For this reason, key is sometimes referred to as tonality, which is an equally good term. As an example, try singing or playing the first seven notes of a major scale (see page 186). The scale doesn't sound finished when you end on the seventh note. You need to add the eighth (tonic) note to resolve things and finish off the scale.

The reasons for this are complicated. Yes, it has something to do with the way we are used to hearing scales performed, but, more importantly, it has a lot to do with the way we are conditioned to experience music throughout our lives. When you started singing the scale you actually established a key. The first three or four notes would have been enough to trigger a network of associations in your brain – or the brain of anyone listening – that oriented you musically, that gave you a sense of which note was the tonic, or 'home'. One could argue that the essence and complexity of music itself can be attributed to the relationship between notes and chords that are closer to home and notes and chords that are, to various degrees, further from home.

 Singing around the tonic

To illustrate the various degrees of 'home' that can be expressed within a key, try this rather simplistic exercise: sing or play the first seven notes of a major scale just as you did earlier, but this time jump down to sing the third note of the scale immediately after the seventh. By ending on the third degree of the scale, you are ending on a note that sounds more final than the seventh note and less final than the first (tonic) note. If you are struggling to hear these different levels of finality, try singing or playing through the scale a few more times, alternating between the first, third and seventh note endings. You should be able to hear that the seventh note ending sounds unresolved, as though the line you have sung has been left hanging. You should also be able to hear that the version of the scale ending on the third note would sound more complete – more finalised – if you added one further note after the third; the first note of the scale, that is, the tonic.

key and scale

If a piece of music has a tonic note of G, it can be said to be in the key of G. But that's not the full story. Musicians distinguish between two different types of key: major and minor. A piece of music in the key of G major will predominantly use notes that are in the scale of G major while a piece in the key of G minor will predominantly use the notes contained in a G minor scale. In either case, these notes are called the diatonic notes in the keys of G major and G minor respectively. Diatonic notes are the notes we expect to hear in the context of a key. The diatonic notes in the key of A major, for example, are A, B, C♯, D, E, F♯ and G♯, the same notes contained in an A major scale (see page 191). If we are playing through a passage of music in the key of A major and come across an E♭ and an A♯, we can describe those two notes as non-diatonic because they are not found in the A major scale. The inclusion of a non-diatonic note in a passage of music will often sound unexpected or jarring to the listener.

Just as there are diatonic notes – notes we would expect to hear in a given key – there are also diatonic chords. Sticking with the example key of A major, we can construct the seven diatonic chords of the key by building a triad on each degree of the A major scale. Each triad must contain a root, a third and a fifth that are diatonic notes in the key of A major.

In addition to major and minor scales, the diatonic chords in selected keys are listed in the appendix.

To construct the tonic chord, we must take the tonic note, A, as the root of the chord. To find the third of the triad we take two steps up the A major scale from the tonic note, and to find the fifth of the triad we take another two steps. This leaves us with the notes A, C♯ and E , the root, third and fifth of the tonic chord. As you might expect, these notes comprise an A major chord.

To construct the chord based on the second degree of the scale – chord II in the key of A major – we must take the second note of the scale as our root. We find the third and the fifth notes in the same way as before, by taking the note that is two steps up the A major scale from the root, and the note that is two steps up again. This leaves us with the notes B, D and F♯, the root, third and fifth of chord II. These notes comprise a B minor chord.

To save you some time, here are A major's seven diatonic chords:

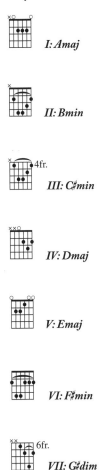

I: Amaj

II: Bmin

III: C♯min

IV: Dmaj

V: Emaj

VI: F♯min

VII: G♯dim

Because the intervals between diatonic notes are the same in any major key, chord I will always be a major chord, chord III will always be a minor chord, chord VII will always be a diminished chord and so on. So we can very easily figure out the seven diatonic chords in the key of C major by following the same pattern, only this time using a C major scale as our basis.

Here are C major's seven diatonic chords:

I: Cmaj

II: Dmin

III: Emin

IV: Fmaj

V: Gmaj

VI: Amin

VII: Bdim

For a chord to be diatonic its every note must be diatonic, not just the root.

key in action

It's time to bring our discussion of tonality down to earth by examining some music. Here is the sort of familiar-sounding chord progression you might find in a rock or folk song:

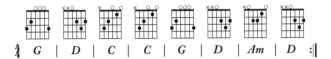

So, in what key is this progression? If you are accustomed to thinking about music in terms of key you will recognise quite quickly that there are only two keys that use these particular chords. For those of us who don't have the benefit of experience, identifying the key of a piece of music can be a more complicated and sometimes confusing process.

A piece of music will usually be eager to establish its key as soon as possible. Most songs begin on the tonic note or chord, and the vast majority end on the tonic note or chord. This is not always the case, so you can't rely on this tendency too much. However, if you encounter a song that begins on an A minor chord, you are entitled to ask, 'Is this song in the key of A minor?'! The first chord of the progression above is G major; does this mean the progression is in the key of G major? The seven diatonic chords of G major are:

This book obeys two conventions for the abbreviation of chord names. The chord of C major might be abbreviated as Cmaj or merely C. The chord of F♯ minor might be abbreviated as F♯min or F♯m. The chord of A major seven might be abbreviated as Amaj7 or AM7, while A minor seven might appear as Amin7 or Am7.

VI: Emin

VII: F♯dim

There seems to be a good match. The first chord of the progression is G major and every chord in the progression is a diatonic chord in the key of G major. Strum through the chord progression a couple of times and try ending the progression on a G major chord. Does the progression sound 'finished' when you end on a G major chord? Hopefully the answer is yes, because this progression is indeed in the key of G major.

A diminished chord contains a diminished 5th rather than the more normal perfect 5th. The third of the chord is a minor 3rd.

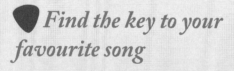

Find the key to your favourite song

Now would be a good time to play through some of the songs you know on the guitar, especially those that use mainly major and minor triads. See if you can identify the keys of these songs and test yourself by ending them on what you believe are their respective tonic chords. Don't worry if you can't identify the key of every song; the identification of keys will become easier with experience.

minor keys

Here is a chord progression in a minor key:

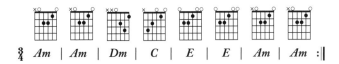

$\frac{3}{4}$ *Am* | *Am* | *Dm* | *C* | *E* | *E* | *Am* | *Am* :‖

No prizes for guessing the key of this progression, which begins and ends on an A minor chord. The scale of A minor consists of the notes A, B, C, D, E, F and G. The diatonic chords of A minor are:

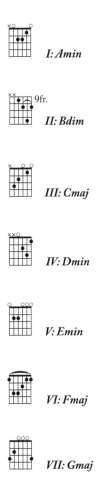

I: Amin

II: Bdim

III: Cmaj

IV: Dmin

V: Emin

VI: Fmaj

VII: Gmaj

There is a problem here. It would seem that the chord progression is not in the key of A minor after all. The chord of E major is not a diatonic chord in A minor and it contains a G♯, a non-diatonic note. This chord progression *is* in the key of A minor, however, so what's going on?

There are, in fact, three different minor scales every musician should know:

The scale of A natural minor is described above; A to G with no sharps or flats. The modal name for this scale is A Aeolian.

The scale of A harmonic minor is identical except for the substitution of a sharpened seventh degree, G♯.

The third scale, A melodic minor, isn't really relevant to the discussion here. (For the curious-minded out there, the melodic minor scale contains different notes depending on melodic direction. The ascending version of the A melodic minor scale contains a raised sixth and seventh degree, F♯ and G♯, which are naturalised when the scale descends.)

So when you encounter a piece of music in a minor key, don't be surprised to find a raised seventh, especially as part of chord V. There are countless songs that include a chord V in its major form.

watch out!

To avoid any confusion at this point, it is worth pointing out that musicians do not distinguish between natural, harmonic and melodic minor keys. In other words, you should never refer to a piece of music as being in the key of F harmonic minor or C♯ natural minor; you should simply refer to the key of F minor or C♯ minor. In any case, always be prepared to come across the raised seventh note and that major chord V in particular.

What are modes?

A full discussion of modes and modality is beyond the scope of this book; there are few songs in the canon of modern popular music that are truly modal. It is a great shame that the writers of instructional guitar magazines habitually dispense misinformation about modality amid the useful information they provide on other, less theoretical subjects. Successive generations of guitarists and guitar teachers have been persuaded to take an interest in an area of music theory - modality - that has little or no relevance to their musical aspirations. The resulting confusion is so profound that there are thousands of guitarists around the world who are, at this very moment, convinced they are playing a piece of music that is modal when, in actual fact, they are playing a piece of music that is conventionally diatonic and not modal at all!

This is not to say that understanding modality is inessential. As a composer, it is very important that you acquire an understanding of modality sooner rather than later in your career. There is no better way to acquire this understanding than to get hold of a resource - be it a book, a teacher or a website - that will explain modality with respect to the keyboard rather than the guitar.

waaait a minute...

Some observant readers will have noticed that the keys of A minor (page 21) and C major (page 18) share all of their diatonic notes and chords. The key of A minor is known as the relative minor of C major for this reason. One could also describe C major as the relative major of A minor. We'll be seeing more of relative minor/major relationships later on.

back to chords

As a guitarist, you probably know all sorts of chords in addition to plain old major and minor. Minor seventh chords, fifth chords, sus4 chords, add9 chords... that sort of thing. This book isn't intended to be a chord reference book, but your career as a songwriter is much more likely to take off if you understand how chords are constructed and how they fit into a piece of music.

We have already seen how basic triads are constructed; a root note is chosen, a note that is a major or minor 3rd above the root note is added and finally a note that is a perfect 5th above the root note is added. That covers major and minor chords, but what about the others?

Chords in general can be defined by the intervallic relationship between the root note and the other note or notes in a chord. So long as you know the rules that govern each chord type you will always be able to build up a chord from the root note alone. Let's start with the easiest chord type, the '5' chord.

A '5' chord consist of a root note and a note that's a perfect 5th above it; that's it! So E5 consists of the notes E and B. The chord of D♭5, to take another example, consists of the notes D♭ and A♭. With the help of the guide to intervals on pages 42-45 you should be able to build any '5' chord.

Here is a guide to the construction of some common chord types:

5 chord: *Consists of two notes: 1. the root note and 2. a note a perfect 5th above the root.*

maj chord: *Consists of three notes, a major triad: 1. a root note, 2. a note a major 3rd above the root and 3. a note a perfect 5th above the root.*

min chord: *Consists of three notes, a minor triad: 1. root, 2. a note a minor 3rd above the root and 3. a note a perfect 5th above the root.*

sus4 chord: *Consists of three notes: 1. root, 2. a note a perfect 4th above the root and 3. a note that's a perfect 5th above the root.*

maj7th chord: *Consists of four notes: a major triad with the addition of a note that's a major 7th above the root.*

min7th chord: *Consists of four notes: a minor triad with the addition of a note that's a minor 7th above the root.*

7th chord: *Consists of four notes: a major triad with the addition of a note that's a minor 7th above the root.*

aug (short for augmented) chord: *Consists of three notes: 1. root, 2. a note a major 3rd above the root and 3. a note that's an augmented 5th above the root.*

dim (short for diminished) chord: *Consists of three notes: 1. root, 2. a note a minor 3rd above the root and 3. a note a diminished 5th above the root.*

dim7th (short for diminished seventh) chord: *Consists of four notes: a diminished chord with the addition of a note that's a diminished 7th above the root.*

maj9th chord: *Consists of five notes: a maj7th chord with the addition of a note that's a major 9th above the root.*

min9th chord: *Consists of five notes: a min7th chord with the addition of a note that's a major 9th above the root.*

9th chord: *Consists of five notes, a seventh chord with the addition of a note that's a maj9th above the root.*

maj11th chord: *Consists of six notes: a maj9th chord with the addition of a note that's a perfect 11th above the root.*

min11th chord: *Consists of six notes: a min9th chord with the addition of a note that's a perfect 11th above the root.*

11th chord: *Consists of six notes: a ninth chord with the addition of a note that's a perfect 11th above the root.*

maj13th chord: *Consists of seven notes: a maj11th chord with the addition of a note that's a major 13th above the root.*

min13th chord: *Consists of seven notes: a min11th chord with the addition of a note that's a major 13th above the root.*

13th chord: *Consists of seven notes: an 11th chord with the addition of a note that's a major 13th above the root.*

add9 chord: *Consists of four notes: a major triad with the addition of a note that's a major 9th above the root.*

min7♭5 chord: *Consists of four notes: a diminished triad with the addition of a note that's a minor 7th above the root.*

6th chord: *Consists of four notes: a major triad with the addition of a note that's a major 6th above the root.*

 The root note

The root note is by far the most important in determining a chord's harmonic function. For example, the substitution of a 7th, min9th or aug5th chord for a conventional major or minor triad will stand the greatest chance of succeeding when both chords are built on the same root note.

---

diatonic chords 'seventh-ified'

The diatonic chords we encountered earlier were triads, chords consisting of three notes, each note a minor or major 3rd higher than the last. If we add another major or minor 3rd on top of these diatonic triads we will turn each chord into a seventh chord of some sort, either a 7, min7 or maj7. The added note should, of course, be a diatonic note of the key in question. Chords consisting of four notes are called tetrads.

Taking the key of A major as an example, the seventh-ified chords would be:

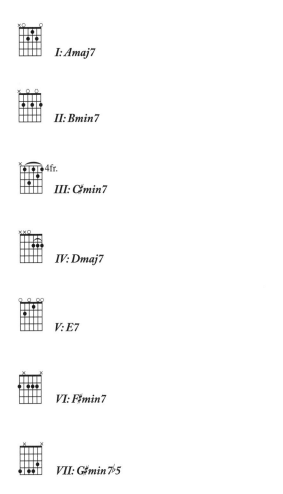

I: Amaj7

II: Bmin7

III: C♯min7

IV: Dmaj7

V: E7

VI: F♯min7

VII: G♯min7♭5

These chords are diatonic chords in the key of A major. Strictly speaking, any chord composed of the diatonic notes of a given key is a diatonic chord in that key. What's important about these seventh-ified chords is that they function in the same way as the triads on which they are based. So the chord of Dmaj in a piece of music in the key of A major could be replaced by a Dmaj7 chord. Dmaj and Dmaj7 would provide different flavours in this context, but they would both fulfil the same harmonic function, they would both be a sort of chord IV.

Later on we will see that chords I to VII in a given key can not only be seventh-ified, they can be ninth-ified, eleventh-ified and thirteenth-ified, too. As a songwriter, you mustn't pay too much attention to the sort of jazz harmony and music theory in general that is to be found in many of the magazines and books aimed at guitarists. These publications tend to mystify harmony (jazz harmony in particular) and can often give the impression that the inclusion of min13 or b9sus chords in a piece of music necessarily increases its harmonic sophistication. While there are some pieces of jazz that are remarkably complex, usually the exotic chords encountered in jazz are functioning in the same way as their diatonic triad equivalents. The chord of A maj11 in the key of A major will function in the same way as the tonic triad, for example.

Help! I've run out of fingers!

Every sort of ninth, 11th and 13th chord contains more than four notes, but that doesn't mean you need to tie your left hand up in knots by including every note. Important notes to include are the root, third and seventh. You could, for example, play a 13th chord by playing four notes rather than all seven; root, third, seventh and thirteenth. In this case you would be leaving out the fifth, ninth and eleventh notes.

so when does the songwriting start?

In just a moment. The purpose of this chapter has been to give you an overview of chord construction and key. If a lot of the information in this chapter is new to you, don't be too hard on yourself and expect to implement it successfully straight away. The following chapters should help things come into focus. Every time you play or write a piece of music you should think about the constitution of chords and the key of the music, even if things are still a little fuzzy.

chapter two:
the riff

As a guitarist, you know all about riffs. From The Beatles' 'Day Tripper' to Metallica's 'Enter Sandman', there are countless songs that are defined by a cool guitar riff. The typical recurring guitar riff is a succession of pentatonic or blues scale notes in the guitar's lower register, sometimes interspersed with chords and usually lasting no longer than two bars. The use of recurring motif as a compositional device is nothing new, and although there is no motivic material in the music of J. S. Bach or Vivaldi that could strictly be called a riff, there are some examples that come reasonably close. The two outer movements of Bach's *Brandenburg Concerto no. 3* use ritornello form, a form in which a passage of instrumental material keeps coming back in a hook-like way.

For the purpose of a discussion about songwriting, the term 'motif' is preferable to 'riff.' It has fewer guitaristic rock/metal connotations and it can be used to describe a broader variety of material. One might hesitate to describe the piano part that opens Coldplay's 'Trouble' as a riff, for example.

A catchy motif can act as the signature of a song, an instantly recognisable instrumental morsel that appears at the start of proceedings as though a song is identifying itself to the listener. Imagine Jimi Hendrix's 'Crosstown Traffic' without the kazoo motif, or Derek and the Dominos' 'Layla' without Eric Clapton's famous guitar part. These songs become less identifiable without their signature motif and one could even question whether they would have been successful without one. Because salient instrumental motifs tend to recur throughout the course of a song, they can help a song's structure to cohere and provide a feature that is common to otherwise motivically diverse sections. In other words, if you come up with a really good motif you're halfway to writing a memorable, well-structured song.

The only problem is that cool-sounding, catchy motivic material is not easy to write. The chances are that if you set out to write the perfect instrumental motif you will come up with something that's not quite catchy and interesting enough to recur throughout a song. Either that, or you will come up with something that sounds super-cool on its own, but doesn't really work with the style of the lyrics or the melody or the song overall when it comes down to it. Even if you compose a motif with the intention of building a song around it from scratch (many hip hop artists work in this way, finding a catchy sample from an existing record, adding a drum beat and building the song up from there), the rest of the songwriting process might not be plain sailing.

In this chapter we are going to look at instrumental motifs; what makes them work, what makes them not work. At the very least, this section of the book should have you thinking about motif, line and harmony in a new way.

 ## *What note am I playing?*

Note names are derived from the layout of the piano keyboard. Turn to appendix A (see page 181) for an illustration and a fretboard diagram naming every note on every string up to the thirteenth fret.

minor pentatonic riffs

The traditional rock/blues guitar riff uses notes from the minor pentatonic scale. As you might expect, a pentatonic scale contains five notes per octave (penta = five). The A minor pentatonic scale contains the notes A, C, D, E and G.

Amin pentatonic scale

The notes of the pentatonic scale are often supplemented with 'blue' notes, such as a note an augmented 4th (or diminished 5th) above the tonic and a note that's a major 3rd above the tonic (D♯ and C♯ respectively in the case of A minor pentatonic). Here is the D minor pentatonic riff that begins Cream's 'Sunshine Of Your Love'.

Dmin pentatonic riff from 'Sunshine Of Your Love'

And here is the D minor pentatonic scale:

Dmin pentatonic position 1

The highlighted note is the 'blue' note, G♯ in this case. The famous guitar riff from The Beatles' 'Day Tripper' uses an E minor pentatonic scale with an added 'blue' note, namely G♯, which is a major third above the root note, E. Here is the E minor pentatonic scale with added blue notes, G♯ and A♯:

Emin pentatonic scale with added 'blue' notes

If you are unfamiliar with pentatonic scales, you owe it to yourself as a guitarist to learn the five minor pentatonic positions and improvise with them, adding in 'blue' notes when improvising rock/blues solos and riffs. For convenience, here is F♯ minor pentatonic in all five positions, each one starting on a different degree of the scale.

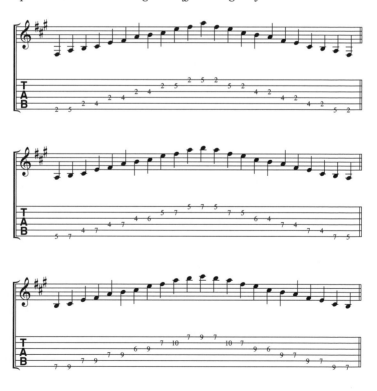

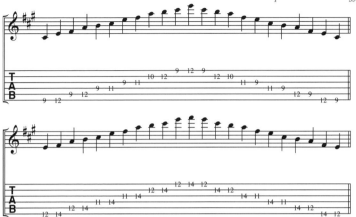

The songs 'Sunshine Of Your Love' and 'Day Tripper' are similar in their use of motifs. Both songs are characterised by a riff derived from the minor pentatonic scale with an added 'blue' note. In both cases the riff continues through the introduction into the verse and recurs in a transposed form.

By contrast, a song such as 'Now I'm Here' by Queen features riffs and riffy chord progressions that are further removed from the conventions of the blues. While there is a prominent blue note (G♯) in the E minor pentatonic riff that acts as an introduction to the verse prior to the entry of the lead vocal, the riff does not recur in a transposed form. The diversity of instrumental material is greater in 'Now I'm Here' in general, and there are a relatively high number of guitaristic ideas throughout. In terms of instrumental material, 'Sunshine Of Your Love' and 'Day Tripper' seem to grow out of a single idea derived from the 'blue' note pentatonic scale, an idea that collaborates with contrasting chord progressions and vocal lines in their respective choruses to create memorable and commercially successful music.

 Can I add blue notes to a major or minor scale?

Yes. Blue notes evoke guitaristic, pentatonic blues playing even when placed in the context of a song or genre that is not conventionally guitaristic.

For another good example of an important 'blue' note in a famous riff, check out the iconic chord progression at the start of 'Smoke On The Water' by Deep Purple.

 How do I transpose?

It is often worth transposing a newly-composed riff in order to hear it in a new key. It is possible that you will end up preferring the sound of a riff when it is played in a key other than the one in which it was conceived.

Transposing a riff on the guitar is straightforward; you simply need to move every note in the riff up or down by a certain number of frets. Moving everything up by one fret will transpose a riff up by the interval of a minor 2nd (a semitone). Moving the riff down by four frets will transpose it down by the interval of a major 3rd.

The disadvantage of thinking about transposition in these terms is that it does not require you to be aware of the name of the key to which you are moving, or indeed the name of the key from which you have moved. However, this is nothing to worry about at an early, experimental stage of the songwriting process.

time is running out

In the context of guitar-driven music, motivic material that is not strictly pentatonic will often contain pentatonic inflections. Consider the opening bass riff from 'Time Is Running Out' by Muse:

Bass riff from 'Time Is Running Out'

This piece is in the key of A minor, and the notes used here are more consistent with the scale of A natural minor (see page 44) than they are with a pentatonic scale. The only non-diatonic note is the D♯ in the second bar, which is an augmented 4th above the root note, A. The presence of this D♯ lends a pentatonic 'blue'-note flavour to the riff.

As with all important motivic material, this riff recurs throughout 'Time Is Running Out', just as the motifs we identified in 'Now I'm Here' and 'Day Tripper' recurred. In 'Time Is Running Out', however, the motif transcribed undergoes a process of development; it changes as it recurs. Following the first chorus, the motif appears in a pared-down, bombastic form.

Motif from 'Time Is Running Out'

enter sandman

At the blacker, heavier end of the genre spectrum, Metallica's 'Enter Sandman' provides us with one of the most famous, instantly recognisable guitar riffs of all time. Metallica's use of this motif has a lot to teach us about the use and development of motivic material in songwriting.

The intro to 'Enter Sandman' is characterised by a motif that uses the E minor pentatonic scale, supplemented by a familiar 'blue' note, A♯ (an augmented 4th above the root, E), which falls by a semitone to A. By the time the verse arrives, this motif has gradually developed into its familiar manifestation, the famous riff that recurs at the beginning of each verse.

The augmented 4th 'blue' note that always falls by a semitone is a persistent feature of the instrumental material in 'Enter Sandman' and a feature common to the famous riff's various manifestations. As in 'Day Tripper', motivic material is transposed, but in the case of 'Enter Sandman' the famous motif changes as the song progresses; it develops.

Development

> *Development is an important idea in classical, 'serious music' composition. In a nineteenth-century piano sonata, for instance, melodic and motivic material would go on a journey, passing through more manifestations than we would expect to encounter in a modern popular song.*

implied harmony and arpeggios

It's time to introduce line. Line is not a standard musicological term and you won't find it in a music dictionary, at least not in the sense it's meant here. Here the word 'line' is used to describe the ever-so-important directionality of musical material, the way it moves horizontally. When we encounter a motif, melody or bass line worthy of comment, be ready for the word line to appear.

The most obvious way to analyse the following example is as a series of chords.

So we could say, 'First there's an Emin chord, followed by a Dmaj chord, followed by…' and so on. Although this sort of analysis can be useful, it doesn't tell us much about what's going on horizontally, as the music moves across the page. If we look at the example in terms of line, on the other hand, we might notice that the highest note in each chord progresses through a complete E minor scale, E, F♯, G, A, B, C, D and finally back to E. If we add a new bass line to our example,

we can see that it too progresses through the notes of the E minor scale, only this time it descends through the scale with the notes E, D, C, B, A, G, F♯ and E. This is a good example of contrary motion, in which the highest and lowest lines move in opposite directions.

Line is an important concept for songwriters in general because many of the most successful songs ever written are defined by strong linear material; memorable melodies like 'Somewhere Over The Rainbow', cool bass lines like the one in 'Billie Jean', catchy riffs like… well, you know. But line is an especially important concept for those songwriters who are also guitarists because guitarists are prone to thinking about songs in terms of 'this chord, then that chord, then this chord again…', which is a way of thinking that can easily find its way into the songwriting process.

'Frère Jacques'

To illustrate further the idea of horizontal and vertical relationships, let's look at the traditional French nursery song, 'Frère Jacques', sometimes known as 'Brother John' in the English-speaking world.

This example is transcribed using conventional notation without tablature. If you can't read conventional notation, don't worry. You should still be able to make out basic patterns in the music, noticing whether a succession of notes is going up or down, for example.

You may have noticed that 'Frère Jacques' is a 'round', a piece of music in which different voices sing the same melody, each voice entering at a different time. In this case, a different voice enters every two bars, singing the melody from the beginning. This means that each voice must be horizontally coherent (it must sing the melody) as well as vertically coherent (each voice, while singing the melody, needs to sound good in relation to the voices around it as they sing their own horizontally coherent melody). If you try to write your own round – or any sort of counterpoint – you will find that achieving horizontal and vertical coherence simultaneously is not at all easy.

The greatest exponent of counterpoint is J. S. Bach. It's worth listening to some of Bach's fugues if only to be awestruck by the brilliant composition of multiple voices (voice = any individual line in counterpoint, whether sung or played) that make sense individually as (horizontal) lines and collectively as (vertical) harmonies.

Guitarists can get stuck with their songwriting because they neglect the linear component of music, including the lines inherent to a chord progression.

linear chords

A Gmaj chord consists of three notes, but these do not need to be struck simultaneously for the listener to understand that a Gmaj chord is present in spirit. An instrument like a clarinet or a voice can imply harmony even though it can only produce one note at a time. Try playing through this G major arpeggio:

Gmaj arpeggio

You are playing one note at a time, but they are the three constituent notes of a Gmaj chord. If you come up with a riff in which those three notes are prominent – especially if the riff starts on the note G – the listener will recognise the chord of Gmaj. The well-known guitar motif from Guns N' Roses' 'Sweet Child O' Mine' is a good example of this. Although it is a linear motif, it still informs the listener of its underlying harmonies, leaving the listener in little doubt about the four chords – Dmaj, Cmaj, Gmaj and Dmaj – it implies.

Any chord can be arpeggiated, and if you think of yourself as a jazz guitarist then you should be able to play all sorts of arpeggiated chords; min7♭5 arpeggios, maj13 arpeggios and so on. The rest of us should at least familiarise ourselves with basic major and minor arpeggios, which also serve as good technical exercises.

Gmaj and Gmin arpeggios

Any motif you write will automatically imply an underlying chord or chord progression, and it usually doesn't benefit the songwriting process to aim for a specific harmonic implication – not consciously, anyway. However, being aware that one-note-at-a-time motifs and melodies can have their own harmonic implications will help you think about and analyse other people's music as well as your own.

Crucially, once you are accustomed to the idea of all linear material implying an underlying harmony of some sort you will quickly be able to infer the harmonic implications of line as you compose. For example, a savvy composer would realise even as he wrote the riff in 'Time Is Running Out' that the following chord progression is implied:

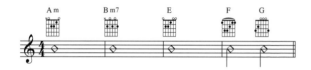

major and minor scales: intervals

As we saw in our discussion of key, an A major scale contains the notes A, B, C♯, D, E, F♯ and G♯.

A major scale

The interval between the first two notes of the scale, A and B, is called a major 2nd. The distance between notes one and three in scale, A and C♯, is the interval of a major 3rd.

Here is a table of the intervallic relationship between the root note, A, and the other notes in the scale:

A to B = major 2nd
A to C♯ = major 3rd
A to D = perfect 4th
A to E = perfect 5th
A to F♯ = major 6th
A to G♯ = major 7th
A to A = perfect octave (8th)

Of course, there are intervals beyond the first octave; 9th, 10th, 11th and so on. These intervals correspond to 2nd, 3rd, 4th, and so on, and are prefixed in the same way with either 'major' or 'perfect' in the context of major scale notes in relation to the root. So we would see the intervals of major 9th, major 10th, perfect 11th, perfect 12th and so on if we continued the scale beyond the first octave.

The advantage of memorising the table above is that it allows you to calculate an interval. If we want to figure out which note is a perfect 5th above G, we only need to play a G major scale through to its fifth note to discover that D is a perfect 5th above G. The ability to calculate intervals is important to any musician, especially when it comes to building chords, which are defined by the intervallic relationships they contain.

You now know how to calculate intervals prefixed by the words 'perfect' and 'major', but what about other intervals? An interval can be called minor, diminished or augmented in addition to major and perfect, so how do we calculate the interval of an augmented 4th, for example?

The first thing to understand is that only certain intervals can be described as major or minor. These are the following:

2nd

3rd

6th

7th

9th (2nd + an octave)

10th (3rd + an octave)

13th (6th + an octave)

14th (7th + an octave)

and so on. You know how to calculate a major 6th from a given note; if you want to calculate a minor 6th you have two options. You can either a) calculate the note that is a major 6th above the given note and then subtract a semitone or b) play the (natural) minor scale of the given note until you get to the sixth note, which will be a minor 6th above the given starting note.

Let's try to work out the note that's a minor 6th above A. The note a major 6th above A is F♯. If we subtract a semitone (that is, move to the note one fret down on the guitar) we arrive at F♮, which, sure enough, is a minor 6th above A. To take the alternative route, we could count six notes up the A natural minor scale,

A natural minor scale

and arrive at F♮ that way.

Here are the intervallic relationships from the tonic, A, to the successive notes in an A minor scale.

A to B = major 2nd
A to C = minor 3rd
A to D = perfect 4th
A to E = perfect 5th
A to F = minor 6th
A to G = minor 7th
A to A = perfect octave (8th)

As you can see, the natural minor scale can be used to calculate the intervals of minor 3rd, minor 6th and minor 7th. If you need to calculate a minor 2nd, that's easy; it's one semitone above a given note. A minor 2nd above C is D♭, a minor 2nd above B is C and so on.

When one of the 'perfect' intervals – that is, 4th, 5th and octave – is altered by the subtraction of a semitone, the resulting interval is not called a minor 4th or minor 5th, it's called a diminished 4th, a diminished 5th. The note a diminished 5th above A is E♭. The note a diminished octave above D is D♭.

Augmented intervals are easier to understand; they apply to 'major'-type intervals like 3rd, 6th and 7th as well as 'perfect' intervals such as 4th and 5th. When an interval is augmented, it means that one semitone has been added to the regular (major or perfect) interval. A major 6th above C is A; an augmented 6th is C to A♯. A perfect 4th above B♭ is E♭; an augmented 4th is B♭ to E.

This section is intended to provide you with a basic understanding of how intervals work, an understanding that will allow you to construct chords and keep up with references to intervals as they appear throughout the book. A thorough discussion of intervals is beyond the scope of this book, and you should seek out a dedicated book about music theory for a complete explanation.

diatonic material

A chord or line is completely diatonic if it contains only the notes we would expect to hear in a given key, notes that constitute the major or minor scale of that key. The famous motif from 'Whiskey In The Jar' by Thin Lizzy is a good example of a motif that uses diatonic notes only.

 A diatonic motif

The main riff from the Led Zeppelin instrumental 'Moby Dick' is a good example of a completely diatonic motif that uses notes from an E minor scale.

Although the riff uses three different pentatonic scales – E minor pentatonic, B minor pentatonic and A minor pentatonic – these three scales are entirely diatonic in this context as they contain notes that can also be found in the E minor scale. This is an important point; motifs based on pentatonic scales can be entirely diatonic. An A minor pentatonic scale contains notes that are also contained in an A minor scale, for example, so a riff that uses notes from the A minor pentatonic scale is entirely diatonic within the key of A minor, or any key in which the five notes of the A minor pentatonic scale are present (A, C, D, E, G); keys such as C major, E minor or D minor. The pentatonic motifs we encountered earlier are not entirely diatonic because they contain 'blue' notes, which cannot be part of the major or minor scale of the tonic key. 'Blue' notes are typical non-diatonic notes, and we'll be seeing more non-diatonic notes and harmonies as we go along.

chromatic material

A chromatic scale is a scale consisting of successive semitones. Here is a two-octave chromatic scale starting on A, ascending and descending. It makes an excellent warm-up exercise.

Chromatic scale

The term 'chromatic' is often used to describe notes and chords that are not diatonic. In the context of the key of C major, an F♯ could be described as a chromatic note. The term chromatic can also be used to describe a series of notes and chords that progress in the same way as a chromatic scale, semitone by semitone.

Many famous riffs and chord progressions are characterised by chromatic movement. The guitar riff from Nirvana's 'Come As You Are' is a good example, as is the opening riff from 'Sunshine Of Your Love'.

The chromatic element common to so many of the most famous guitar riffs and chord progressions is trying to tell us something. Having just the right amount of the unexpected in a passage of music – whether it's an unusual rhythm, a special effect or a moment of chromaticism – is a near-necessity if the passage of music in question is to possess character and memorability.

chapter three:
chord progressions

inversions, dominant chords and harmonic rhythm

How do you begin the process of writing a song? For most guitar-playing songwriters it all starts with a chord progression, a series of chords that seem to go well together, that capture the composer's imagination and cry out for continuation. The archetypal guitar-playing songwriter is the folk songwriter, and the famous folk and folk/rock songs of the 60s and 70s are driven by their chord progressions. Remarkable riffs, instrumental motifs and bass lines are not absent from the output of Bob Dylan, Loudon Wainwright and Neil Young, but the oeuvre of these songwriters is full of chord progressions that have clearly been written at the guitar. Just as the classic rock and metal songs featured in the previous chapter suited an examination of riffs, our analysis of chord progressions will feature examples that are idiomatic of acoustic folk music.

analysing a progression

Few folk songs are more iconic than 'American Pie'. While the following chord progressions are not a transcription of 'American Pie', they have a harmonic rhythm and a vocabulary of chords that will be familiar to anyone who knows Don McClean's classic.

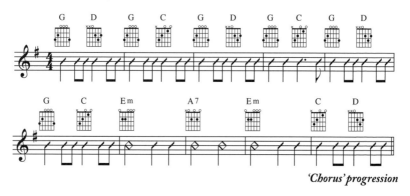

'Chorus' progression

This progression starts on a Gmaj chord and, sure enough, the song is in the key of G major. Now we know the key of the song we can ascribe a numeral to each diatonic chord, just as we did in the 'Key in action' subchapter (see page 18).

The prevalent chords in this progression, chords I, IV and V, are often thought of as the three strongest diatonic chords. The essence of music was described earlier in terms of the tension between notes and harmonies that are close to home, and notes and harmonies that are further from home. In the same terms, we can think of chords I, IV and V as being close to home. Lots of classic chord progressions are based around these chords, such as 'Wild Thing' by The Troggs and 'Knockin' On Heaven's Door' by Bob Dylan. The altered chord II in bar 8 features a non-diatonic note (C♯), making it the most harmonically remote part of the progression, the point furthest from home.

Here is the chord progression from the 'verse' of our song, complete with Roman numerals.

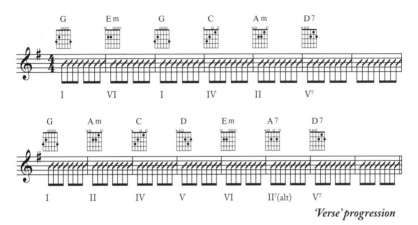

'Verse' progression

You'll notice that the verse and chorus have similar harmonic vocabularies, and it would be safe to describe the song as harmonically unremarkable. The song does not modulate, for example, and it consists entirely of diatonic chords with the exception of the altered chord II that appears in both verse and chorus. Despite this apparent lack of diversity, the verse and chorus are instantly distinguishable, and the average listener would be able to tell which section of the song he was listening to. So what is it that makes the verse and chorus distinct?

The answer is right in front of you, and it's an obvious difference between the 'verse' and 'chorus' progressions; the rate at which chords change. In the 'chorus' progression there are usually two chords per bar, in the 'verse' progression there is usually one chord per bar. The rate of chord change, known as harmonic rhythm, is a very important characteristic of chord progressions and it should be one of the first things you look at when analysing a song. Changes in harmonic rhythm between sections are common and a relatively fast harmonic rhythm during the chorus is typical, as is a relatively slow harmonic rhythm during the bridge or middle-eight.

The next time you find yourself stuck with a song you're writing, consider changing the harmonic rhythm during the bridge or chorus. If nothing else, a change in harmonic rhythm will help to sustain a song's momentum and drive it forwards. A song of above-average length, such as 'Stairway To Heaven' or 'American Pie', needs all the drive and momentum it can get.

 ## G major

There are plenty of folk songs in the key of G major, which might have something to do with the pleasing, full sound of an open Gmaj chord on the guitar. The chord progression that is repeated throughout 'The Times They Are A-Changin'' by Bob Dylan is a good example, an entirely diatonic progression featuring every diatonic triad in the key of G major apart from chords III and VII. Chords III and VII are also absent from the progressions above, and they are the least commonly used diatonic triads in major keys.

the dominant chord

The fifth note in a major or minor scale can be referred to as the dominant, and the triad built on the fifth degree of a major or minor scale (chord V) is often called the dominant chord. The term dominant works in the same way as the term tonic, although tonic refers to the first note or chord of a scale rather than the fifth. The reason for giving the first note or chord of a scale a special name (tonic) should be obvious to you; the first note or chord of a scale is home. But why should we bother with a special name for the fifth chord of a major or minor scale?

The dominant chord (chord V) resolves to the tonic chord (chord I) with more finality than any other triad. Consider reading the previous sentence more than once! To put it another way, the final chord in a piece of music that will best convey a sense of finality is, of course, the tonic chord; but the most conclusive, final-sounding pair of chords you could possibly have would be chord V followed by chord I, dominant

followed by tonic. The dominant chord prepares the listener for the tonic, and in some circumstances following chord V with anything other than chord I can sound quite unexpected.

Take another look at the progressions above, and play them through while paying particular attention to the role of Dmaj and D7 chords. From now on, you should always pay close attention to the key of the music you are playing or composing, alert to the presence of tonic and dominant chords. Chord V is not significant in every song, and in some songs it doesn't appear at all. In a great many songs, however, chord V functions in much the same way as it does here (and in 'The Times They Are A-Changin'' for that matter), preparing the listener for a return home, to the tonic chord.

The (major) third in a dominant chord will want to resolve to the tonic note.

Focus

The dominant chord V and chord V7 – Dmaj and D7 in this case – are both dominant chords, although V7 is usually referred to as a dominant seventh. The dominant seventh chord is important because it orients the listener thanks to the unique intervals it contains, notes a major 3rd and a minor 7th above the root. Try playing a G7 chord, for example, and your ear will understand it as a dominant chord, a chord that wants to resolve to a Cmaj or Cmin tonic.

chord progressions II

The Eagles' 'Hotel California' is worth analysing in its entirety. Even though it is more than six minutes long, the iconic song consists of just two distinct sections, verse and chorus. Here's the verse,

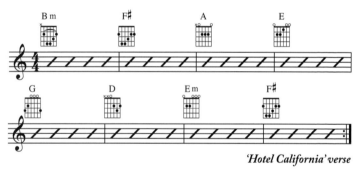

'Hotel California' verse

which leads straight into the chorus,

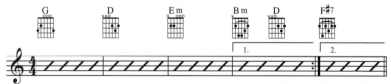

'Hotel California' chorus

The verse is in the key of B minor, and its first six chords are remarkable; look at the intervals separating each chord. We have Bmin to F♯maj, and F♯ is a 5th above B. We then have Amaj to Emaj; E is a 5th above A. Then there's Gmaj to Dmaj. Each pair of chords is suggesting a sort of tonic-to-dominant relationship (the first pair are literally tonic-to-dominant, of course), and each pair is one tone lower than the last. The idea of a repeated I–V relationship is reinforced by the altered chord IV in bar 4, which contains a non diatonic note (G♯). Why would an altered note – a G♯ in place of the diatonic G♮ – reinforce an implied I–V relationship?

more about the dominant chord

We established a moment ago that the dominant chord is the chord that best prepares the listener for the arrival of the tonic; it 'sets up' the tonic chord. Part of this 'setting up' relates to the way the third of the dominant triad (the seventh note in the scale of the key) wants to resolve to the root note of the tonic chord, the tonic note. If you play an open Dmaj chord followed by an open Gmaj chord, for instance, you will be able to hear an F♯ resolve to a G on the top E string.

In order for there to be an effective resolution between these two notes, they must be separated by the interval of a semitone. The third of the dominant must be a major 3rd above the root for it to be able to ascend by one semitone to the root of the tonic. The dominant chord is always a major chord for this reason, even though a natural minor scale would suggest that the diatonic chord V in a minor key should be a minor chord (see page 21).

When we encounter a non-diatonic major or 7 chord like the ones featured in this chapter so far (A7 and Emaj respectively) it's likely that we are dealing with the most common non-diatonic chord, the applied dominant. An applied dominant chord functions as the dominant of a diatonic chord other than the tonic. Chord V is the dominant of chord I, of course, and in the same sense chord VI can function as the applied dominant of chord II, chord VII can function as the applied dominant of chord III and so on. The (non-diatonic) A7 in the 'verse' progression above functions as the applied dominant of the chord that follows it, chord V (Dmaj). In 'Hotel California', the (non-diatonic) Emaj chord in bar 4 is the applied dominant of the chord preceding it, chord VII, Amaj. The non-diatonic notes in both cases are the third of the applied dominant chords, which are altered so as to be one semitone below the note they want to resolve to, D and A respectively.

This is not easy stuff to get your head around. If these concepts are new to you, the idea of an applied dominant might take a while to sink in. It might help to explain the applied dominant in different terms. Let's look at it this way: chord VI in the key of G major would ordinarily be an E minor chord. In order to make a chord that is the applied dominant of chord II (Amin) we need to change our chord VI into a major chord so that it will contain a G♯ that will resolve to the A in Amin. This is exactly why there is a non-diatonic chord in the 'verse' progression above. The A7 chord functions as an applied dominant of Dmaj because it is a variation of chord II containing a C♯ rather than a C♮. The C♯ resolves to the D in the subsequent Dmaj chord.

back to california

The harmonic rhythm of 'Hotel California' is consistent throughout verse and chorus, with the single exception of the Bmin to Dmaj chord change in bar 4 of the chorus. This degree of consistency is unusual in a song of such length. We would be entitled to expect a change in harmonic rhythm analogous to the change we saw between our 'verse' and 'chorus' progressions, with a sustained increase (or decrease) in the rate of chord change in the chorus.

 Varied harmonic rhythm

Check out Leonard Cohen's 'Hallelujah', in which varied harmonic rhythm is an important feature. You will find that the harmonic rhythm slows down during the chorus, for example, and in bar 3 of the verse and bar 1 of the bridge there is a chord change on the last beat of the bar, a variation of harmonic rhythm that sustains the listener's interest.

inversions

There is another concept relating to the construction of chords that should be understood by all musicians; that of inversion.

As you know, basic major and minor chords are triads, chords containing three notes. When the root note of a triad is placed in the bass this is called root position. All of the basic chords we have encountered so far are in root position because they all have their root note at the bottom of the chord. So, our standard open Cmaj chord shape

Cmaj

has a C as its bass note. It is in root position.

A Cmaj chord contains three notes, C, E and G. If we put E, the third of the chord, in the bass

Cmaj/E

are we still looking at a Cmaj chord? Yes. But this time the chord is no longer in root position, it's a first-inversion chord. If we put the fifth of the chord, G, in the bass

Cmaj/G

we still have a Cmaj chord, but this time it's a second-inversion chord. If we were dealing with a more complex chord such as Cmaj13, which might contain seven notes, we could put the root, third or fifth of the chord in the bass to create root position, first-inversion and second-inversion chords respectively, just as we did with Cmaj. Because

Cmaj13 contains more than three notes, though, we could continue putting different notes from the chord in the bass to create more inversions. Putting the seventh of the chord in the bass would give us a third-inversion chord and putting the eleventh of the chord in the bass would give us a fifth-inversion chord, for example.

So what's the big deal, why the special terminology? Well, the bass note has a big impact on the strength and feel of a chord and its surrounding harmonies. If we were to end a piece of music with the tonic chord (as is usual), putting the third of the chord in the bass would make it sound less strong, less final. Putting the fifth in the bass would weaken the chord still further. Then there's the all-important linearity of a chord progression, which has a lot to do with the bass line. Very often the inclusion of first and second-inversion chords in a chord progression helps the bass line to move stepwise and drive the music forwards.

Here are some inversion chords commonly used on the guitar:

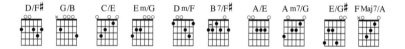

Try modifying one of your songs, replacing a couple of root position chords with inversion chords. Bear in mind that a first-inversion chord is more likely than a (weaker) second-inversion chord to sound good in the context of a progression. You should also bear in mind that the person playing or singing the lowest note in an arrangement is controlling the inversion of a chord, and that person isn't always the guitarist!

Keys and their diatonic chords

Appendix B (see page 185) lists the diatonic chords of several keys.
It includes inversion chords and seventh chords in addition to root-
position chords. It is of particular use to songwriters experimenting
with chord substitutions.

chapter four: chord progressions - hands on!

I SIT DOWN WITH MY GUITAR to write a song. The first chord I strum is an open Cmaj chord and a menu appears in my head as if by magic. It looks like this:

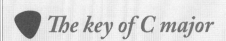

The key of C major

Chord I: C major
Chord II: D minor
Chord III: E minor
Chord IV: F major
Chord V: G major
Chord VI: A minor
Chord VII: B diminished

This is my vocabulary of diatonic chords. I'm going to write a chord progression intended for the verse of my song and I'm going to use diatonic chords. This is going to be a conventional sort of song, so

I'm going to write a verse consisting of a repeated four-bar chord progression with one chord in each bar.

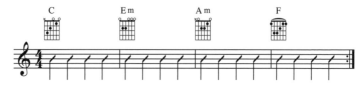

Four-bar progression

 The magic of four

Four-bar and eight-bar chord progressions are typical, as are twelve-bar and sixteen-bar progressions; anything divisible by four sounds 'normal'. The vast majority of chord progressions that are familiar to the average guitarist will consist of four-bar chord progressions, or progressions that are divisible by four bars. For example, 'Hotel California', 'Knockin' On Heaven's Door' and 'Hallelujah' are completely normal in this regard, consisting variously of four-, eight- and sixteen-bar chord progressions.

Strum through the four-bar progression, which, though bland, is a pleasant enough chord progression. For the remainder of this chapter we will look at what can be done to modify and enhance this progression and take it to the next level. Applying different techniques and alterations to a progression will help you to express yourself with greater precision and originality.

transposition

As soon as a chord progression is written it's a good idea to try it out in a few different keys. Transposing a progression to a different key will not only change the flavour of the chord progression, it will open up new possibilities in terms of the way it can be played and modified on the guitar. Most importantly, different keys suit different voices, so finding the right key for your voice (or your singer's voice) is crucial.

Our four-bar progression is entirely diatonic, so transposition is straightforward; chords I, III, VI and IV are easily transferred to another key. If we wanted to transpose our progression to the key of G major, for example, we need only play chords I, III, VI and IV in that key. Here comes that magical menu again...

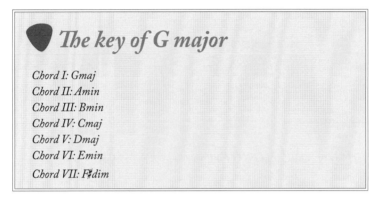

The key of G major

Chord I: Gmaj
Chord II: Amin
Chord III: Bmin
Chord IV: Cmaj
Chord V: Dmaj
Chord VI: Emin
Chord VII: F♯dim

So our transposed chord progression would look like this:

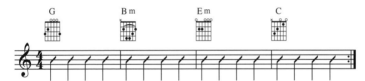

Chords I–VII in a number of major keys can be found in the appendix. Try transposing this chord progression to other major keys to find out which key sounds right to you and which keys are most guitaristic. Certain keys – E♭ major, for example – are not particularly well suited to the guitar in that they restrict the availability of open chords and open strings.

There is another, foolproof way of transposing a chord progression. Dust off your capo, strap it somewhere across your fretboard and play the original chord progression in this new position. While there are many well-known songs that use a capo, perhaps the most obvious example is 'Here Comes The Sun' by The Beatles.

Hang on, what's a capo?

A capo is a simple device that attaches to a guitar neck and holds down all of the strings on a fret of your choice, thereby shortening the length of the strings and raising their pitch. You could do the same thing by barring a fret with your first finger as you would if you were playing a conventional Fmaj chord, but then your first finger would be out of action and the remaining fingers of your left hand would have limited reach. A capo is a very useful tool and an essential purchase for any guitarist.

changing linearity: inversions

Returning to our four-bar progression, we are going to look at what is perhaps the most important linear component of any chord progression, the bass line. Play through the progression again, then play the lowest note in each chord in order: C, E, A and F. There's nothing remarkable here, but by experimenting with the inversion of the chords we might arrive at a bass line that adds something valuable to the progression. Here's an example:

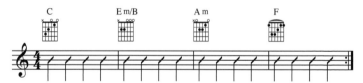

The only alteration is to the second chord, Emin. An Emin triad consists of the notes E, G and B. Originally the root note of the chord (E) was in the bass, which means the chord was in root position. By putting the fifth of the triad (B) in the bass we have created a second-inversion E minor chord. If we had put the third of the triad (G) in the bass we would have created a first-inversion chord.

Play through our altered four-bar progression, then play the four bass notes in order: C, B, A and F. The progression has a different feel now because we have invoked a common songwriting technique, the descending bass line. The notes C, B and A proceed incrementally down the C major scale and create the familiar sound of a descending chord progression. Numerous classic songs feature prominent descending bass lines, such as 'I Want You' by Bob Dylan and 'Something' by The Beatles.

Here is a modification of our four-bar progression in which the first and last chords of the progression have become first-inversion chords.

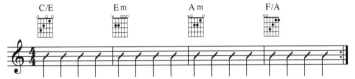

The bass line is more static now, consisting of the notes E and A only. The chord progression no longer sounds as strong as it did in its original, entirely root-position form. The first-inversion chords have added ambiguity to the progression.

As you experiment with inversions you will quickly gain a sense of what first- and second-inversion chords can add to your compositions. You will probably find that first-inversion chords can be added to an existing progression with relative ease, while second-inversion chords are a bit more tricky. The brilliant and underrated indie singer-songwriter Elliott Smith uses second-inversion chords remarkably often in his music, for example, but you may find that a preponderance of root-position chords is just what you need if you are aiming at something more conventional.

the top line

The bass line and the vocal line are typically the most important linear elements of a song. For this reason, there is a lot to be said for the practice of writing a song with a bass guitar on your lap, picking out a bass line while singing a melody, prioritising the outer parts and allowing these lines to dictate the composition of a song. It seems probable that many of Paul McCartney's songs began life in this way. At the very least, McCartney's songs exhibit a sharp awareness of the interplay between the vocal line and the bass line, and he seems to think in a more obviously 'linear' way than most songwriters.

Having composed a worthy chord progression, a songwriter will occasionally find himself unable to invent a melody it will accommodate. What can you do in this situation?

Start by looking again at your chord progression. In our case, we will continue with our original four-bar progression. Play through the chords again, but this time concentrate on the highest note in each chord. You will notice that the top line of the progression is very static, comprising the notes E, E, E and F.

Play it through once more, only this time strum or pick the chords in such a way that the top (thin) E string is omitted. Now the notes on the B string – C, B, C and C – comprise the top line.

The purpose of this exercise is to create a top line that might just inspire a vocal melody and enhance the progression itself. The top lines we have come up with so far are rather static and uninspiring, but if we get a bit more inventive with our chords we should be more successful. This time we will aim for contrary motion between the bass line and the top line. In other words, when the bass line moves down, the top line moves up, and when the bass line moves up, the top line moves down.

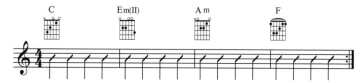

The second chord is still Emin, but the third of the triad, G, is now the highest note. If we look at the top line and the bass line side by side...

TOP LINE: E (up to) G (down to) E (up to) F

BASS LINE: C (down to) E (up to) A (down to) F

...we can see that contrary motion has been achieved.

There is nothing particularly special or desirable about having contrary motion between the outer parts, but it is something composers and songwriters have been doing – consciously – for centuries. While the E–G–E–F melody we have arrived at is certainly not an amazing melody in itself, there might be one small element of it that appeals to you (the initial rise from E to G perhaps), which could inspire a vocal melody.

 ## Hang on, what is bass?

The bass note is the lowest note in a given chord. The bass line is the line produced by a succession of bass notes in a chord progression, for example. In a band, the bassline is usually played by the bass guitar; this is not to deny your prerogative as a songwriter to decide the inversion of each chord and, if necessary, to dictate the exact line your bassist will play.

changing harmony - seventhification

Okay, that's a silly made-up word too far. This is where we consider the possibility of modifying our progression by 'seventhifying' one or two of the chords.

As soon as I mention the number seven, yet another drop-down menu magically appears listing the diatonic chords of our key (C major) in their seventhified form.

 ## The key of C major

Chord I7: Cmaj7
Chord II7: Dmin7
Chord III7: Emin7
Chord IV7: Fmaj7
Chord V7: G7
Chord VI7: Amin7
Chord VII7: Bmin7b5

If we were to replace the chords in our progression with their '7' equivalents, this would be the result:

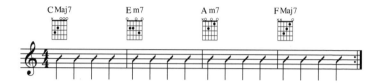

The seventhified progression would suit some genres better than others. We would certainly be leaving folk, pop and rock behind us somewhat by composing a verse chord progression consisting only of min7 and maj7 chords. The inclusion of one of those seventhified chords in our progression, however, might sound rather good in any genre.

To my ear the best chord to seventhify would be the last one, Fmaj. Play through the original progression again, replacing Fmaj with Fmaj7. Can you see why I like the sound of this particular modification? Here's a clue: it has something to do with the top line.

The top line of the original progression was E, E, E and F. With the Fmaj7 chord replacing Fmaj, the top line has the opportunity to become E, E, E and E; E being a note common to all four chords. Although we were trying to make the top line less static earlier, there is something effective about one or two notes that appear in every chord in a progression, something that glues the progression together. Check out 'Wonderwall' by Oasis, a song in which the two top notes of the rhythm guitar part remain the same throughout the verse, and, indeed, throughout the entire song.

In the spirit of Oasis, let's try to glue our chord progression together by having two notes that appear in every chord, the E at the top and one other note. If you play through the first two chords of our progression, Cmaj and Emin, you should notice that the chords have an obvious note in common aside from the top E, namely the G of the open G string. What happens if we include an open G string in every chord in addition to an open E string?

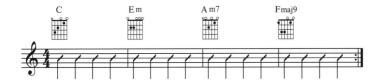

Play through this progression a couple of times and see what you think. The inclusion of the open G string has turned Amin into Amin7 while Fmaj has become Fmaj9 thanks to the E (seventh) and G (ninth) notes which have been added to the F, A and C (root, third and fifth) of the original Fmaj triad.

(Don't worry if you are unable to identify a rather complex chord like Fmaj9 from the notes alone at this point. With practice you'll be able to identify chords in the blink of an eye. For the purposes of songwriting and composition at the guitar, knowing the name of a chord is often relatively unimportant.)

Experiment with your own chord progressions by adding a little 'glue'. If you find two consecutive chords in a progression that have a note in common, see if you can include that note in other nearby chords.

other altered harmony

There are other ways to modify the progression by altering its chords. For example, we could experiment by adding 9-type chords as well as 7-type chords to the progression.

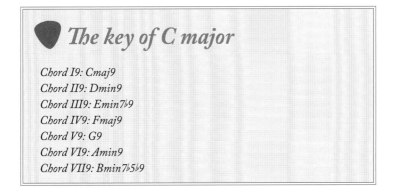

The key of C major

Chord I9: Cmaj9
Chord II9: Dmin9
Chord III9: Emin7♭9
Chord IV9: Fmaj9
Chord V9: G9
Chord VI9: Amin9
Chord VII9: Bmin7♭5♭9

Try replacing one of the chords in the progression with a 9 chord, replacing Amin with Amin9, for instance. Of course, you could do the same thing with 11 chords, 13 chords, add9 chords or sus4 chords, experimenting with various substitutions until you find a combination you like. This is a clumsy way of working and it would be a bad idea to start cycling through a selection of possible substitute chords every time you compose at the guitar. Every now and again, though, you will compose yourself into a corner, and having a few alternative chords up your sleeve could prove useful.

suspension

One interesting way of sprucing up a chord progression is suspension, a technique whereby a note from one chord is 'suspended' into the following chord. In order for a true suspension to take place, the note that is suspended should be one that is alien to the second (following) chord and it should at some point resolve downwards to a note that is part of the second chord. Here is a good example of a suspension within the context of our four-bar progression:

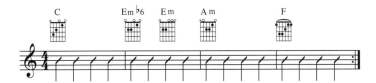

In this example the C on the B string from the initial Cmaj chord is held over for the first two beats of the following Emin chord. It then resolves downwards to an open B string, leaving a clean Emin chord that plays for the final two beats of the second bar.

● *What's the difference between an added-note chord and a suspension chord?*

An added note is played in addition to the notes of a chord, while a suspension replaces the note in the chord to which it wants to resolve. For example, Cadd4 contains an E (the third of the chord), whereas Csus4 does not.

Traditionally, a suspension is a tone or semitone above the resolution note, though sometimes the term is used to describe the suspension of a note below the resolution note; in Csus2, for example, the suspended second (D) is included instead of the third (E) to which it wants to resolve.

The question you may find yourself asking at this point is: why interpret the progression in this way? Why not simply say that the second bar contains two chords, Emin♭6 (which features the notes E, G, B and C) followed by Emin?

There is absolutely no reason why you shouldn't think of bar 2 in this way. It is not necessary to involve the word 'suspension' at all. In this case, however, the idea of suspension is useful because it tells us something about the way the listener will perceive the chord progression in bars 1 and 2. Play through those bars again. The chances are that you experience the note C at the start of bar 2 as a hangover from the previous Cmaj chord, as a suspension. The chances are that you experience a small feeling of satisfaction or relief when the C resolves to B in the middle of bar 2. For these reasons, the term suspension is the correct one here.

As a side note, sus4 chords are so called because they imply a suspension, a fourth that wants to resolve downwards to the third of a normal major or minor triad. Play through this brief progression and you'll understand.

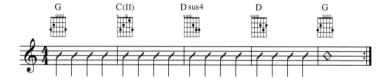

For a sus4 chord to effect a suspension in a strict, technical sense it is necessary for the fourth of the 'suspension chord' to have been present in the previous chord. The G that is the sus4 note in the Dsus4 chord in the progression above, for example, is also present in the preceding Cmaj chord.

Where else can I use suspensions?

In the context of a chord progression it is common for a note that is part of one chord to be held over into a second, subsequent chord; this is the basis of suspension. Experiment by including just such a held-over note in the vocal line of your songs.

songwriter interview: eric bazilian

Eric Bazilian is an American songwriter, singer, instrumentalist and producer who has achieved success both as a founding member of The Hooters and as an industry songwriter. He has written songs for artists and bands such as Cyndi Lauper, Robbie Williams, Scorpions, Journey, Ricky Martin and Jon Bon Jovi. His most famous song is probably 'One of Us', which was a massive hit for Joan Osborne in 1995.

Artists, writers and musicians in general often create a space for themselves that is conducive to their work. Is your location important to you?

It seems to be. I think you need to have your home sanctuary, but at the same time I think you need to have changes of venue. I have a studio, which is my sanctuary, and I tend to get most of my ideas there. However, I like setting up satellite spaces, too. For example, I live in Sweden in the summer, and for a while I was working in my in-laws' barn there. It was a total mess and they literally cleared just a few square metres for me to work in, and I had an incredible burst of creativity there. A few summers later, I moved into a different building on the same property and I had another incredible burst of creativity.

So, yes, location is important. I've heard of people having revelatory 'song visitations' standing on the edge of the Grand Canyon, envisioning an entire song. Or people in a near-death situation... I've never had that, for me songs tend to come when I'm looking for them.

So in order for you to be the quite prolific songwriter that you are do you have to be disciplined about making time, saying to yourself 'for the next two hours I'm going to go into the studio and write a song whether I feel like it or not'?

Yes, I absolutely do. Usually if I write a song when I'm not feeling like it, it's not good. I sort of have to coax it along. But that doesn't mean that writing a song when I don't feel like it isn't important. Even if it's garbage, it's clearing the pipes. I can think of a few examples where that's worked out really well, where I've written something that I knew was garbage while it was coming out and the next day something magical happens. I think today I'm going to go and do that, in fact.

It's one of those bad days!

I don't know. The thing is, you never know. I find that clearing the pipes in this way is also important when it comes to collaborative songwriting. It's vital that I'm able to do some solitary writing prior to a collaboration because if I don't get the chance to sit by myself and free associate and get ideas then I'm worthless in a group situation.

When you say collaborative writing –

I mean when other people are in the room, although I have done some writing where people have provided me with lyrics and I find that incredibly fulfilling. When they're good lyrics, that's the easiest thing in the world. I wish I could do that for a job!

Would you say that writing lyrics is harder for you than writing the music, then?

To write really meaningful lyrics is much harder. It's like a story. I think it's different if you're writing for something and you have a particular story that you want to tell. For example, Jennifer Brook and I did the theme for *The Dollhouse* TV series. Now, the theme that's on the show is instrumental, but the producers also wanted a full-length song. So just when we thought, 'oh great, this is the best half-hour we've ever spent', they said, 'part of the deal is that we get a full-length song'. In that case it wasn't so hard because we knew that we were going to write something that paralleled the story in the show, and we knew what that was. So it was just a case of storytelling; it's easier to tell a story if you know what it is, is what I'm trying to say.

But usually a song doesn't conform to an extrinsic narrative.

Exactly. I'm usually a free-associative writer, so I want to write songs about man's inhumanity to man, or the tragedy in Haiti. If I have something on my mind and I just let my mind go it'll usually end up back there. Or sometimes I'll end up revisiting some incident from my distant past that I've forgotten. It's very therapeutic in that way.

Sometimes people think of a songwriter for established artists as being the sort of composer who is a bit cynical in the way he goes about writing a song, trying to come up with something commercial at all costs. But you seem to treat songwriting as a highly personal process.

When it's good, it's personal. The best songs I've written – not just artistically, but commercially – have been songs that were no effort, songs that were a story waiting to be told.

Would it be fair to say that 'One Of Us' is your most commercially successful song?

Isn't that ironic, because that song is also the biggest and most direct window into my brain, my soul. Would you like to know how that song was written?

In 1994 Rob Hyman, Rick Chertoff and I were actively writing songs for Joan Osborne. At that time I was living in a town house outside Philadelphia with my new girlfriend from Sweden. We shared one car at the time and she would drop me off at the studio. I remember vividly leaning over and picking up Rob's guitar, a cherry red 1965 Gibson ES330, and, as often happens, a riff came out. It was a little arpeggiated riff in E minor, and it had a major 7th over the second chord, which was a C. I remember playing this riff thinking, 'wow, this riff is unique'. I asked Rob to record it. The next day I came back and I said, 'can you remember that riff, do you still have that riff somewhere?' because I'd forgotten how it went! Rob couldn't find it. I was very disappointed, but later on that afternoon he had his headphones on and he said, 'I've found the riff! I had labelled it "mandolin riff".' Thank god he had archived it because he played it back for me, I started playing it and I played it all day, played it on the guitar, played it on the piano. My girlfriend came to pick me up that afternoon, and when she walked in – I have a clear picture of this – I was sitting at the piano playing that riff and Joan was sort of scatting over it.

So my girlfriend and I went home, we had dinner and we decided to watch *The Making Of Sgt Pepper*, which came on TV, and I had never seen it before. When it ended, she was fascinated by the multitrack recording technology, the four-track technology George Martin was using at Abbey Road. I said to my girlfriend that that pile of wires in the dining room is a four-track recorder. 'Record something for me,' she said. So, the easiest thing for me to do was to set up a little drum pattern on my keyboard sampler, play some bass notes, and double the guitar part with an electric piano. What I thought was, ok, I'll play the 'mandolin riff' for an intro on the guitar, then for the verse I'll just arpeggiate the chords, then I did a little 'B' section to break it up, eight bars, no I think I'll make it six bars, it's a little more interesting that way. Then I came up with another section, a Beatles-influenced instrumental bridge, that didn't make it into the final Joan Osborne version. So I recorded all of that music, that and the electric guitar, onto two of the four tracks simultaneously. I played it back for her and thought she'd be very impressed. She said, 'well, that's very nice, but now you have to sing it'. At this point, 90 per cent of my songwriting had been collaborative, and I said 'silly girl, don't you know that to write a song you have to have a concept, a chorus, and write verses, and when you write good verses you have to question your chorus, and change it, and then write new verses and realise that the chorus was better before, and then rewrite the verses, and so you finally reach consensus?' 'Okay,' she said, 'fine,' and she fell asleep on the sofa.

About two minutes after that I was listening to the track in the headphones. I heard the voice of Brad Robertson, of the Crash Test Dummies, in my head. It was singing, [sings] 'if God had a name'. So I thought, I've written a couple of songs to bible stories before, I'm putting it on record, I'm going in. So I started singing, and the verses came out on the first pass, I punched in the chorus on the second pass and that's what came out. You've heard it a million times, the song wrote itself. The song was there, I happened to be there at the time to catch it.

You didn't need to rewrite the verse, rework the chorus because it didn't fit with the verse, you didn't run into any walls...

I didn't change a word. You know, Neil Young put out a record, it was a live recording from 1968. He tells some great stories and one is about songwriting where he talks about 'Mr. Soul', a song he did with Buffalo Springfield. He says something like, 'This song took about as long to write as the song is. I only wrote it once unlike most of the songs I've written. I never changed a word because I never needed to change a word. Any songwriter will tell you, sometimes that's just how they come, and often those are the best ones.'

Anyway, we presented the demo to Joan and said, 'Joan, would you like to sing it?', and Joan couldn't easily say no. She had to say yes! So I wrote the words out for her, ran through the melody. We did a live to DAT recording, electric guitar and vocal and that was that. I knew then that the planets were aligned.

When exactly did you have that feeling that this was something that would have mass appeal, that you had really nailed something? Was it at the stage of the 'Crash Test Dummies' demo?

I knew that I'd written something special, something personal at that point. I knew it was something that I would always be proud of, that I'd told my story well. It wasn't until I heard Joan's voice coming back at me that I knew the song had found its voice.

It was similar to when we did 'Girls Just Wanna Have Fun' with Cyndi Lauper. I didn't write that song, Robert Hazard wrote that song. Rick Chertoff just had this feeling that this song would be a good one for Cyndi Lauper to do. Rob Hyman and I were her band on that record; I played the guitars on it and he played the keyboard. We spent months in pre-production going through songs that Rick had found for her. She didn't do much writing on that album, I think she wrote four of the songs. But Rick had it in his head that 'Girls Just Wanna Have Fun' was going to be a Cyndi Lauper song. His original version was very New Wave-y. It was much faster, more like [plays and sings faster, more aggressive-sounding version]. Cyndi quite frankly hated it, and I wasn't much of a fan of the song either, but it did have a great title and it did have kind of a hooky chorus. We tried all different ways of recording it, of demoing it. We tried to do it rock and roll, it wasn't working. We tried to do it Cat Stevens; that certainly wasn't working. One day when we were really ready to give up on it we were talking about how much we loved 'Come On Eileen', which was big at that time. It really was a great record, the Celtic thing with the violin, the banjo, it all really worked. Cyndi said, 'Can you make it sound like "Come On Eileen"?', so I thought about it for a second and I said, you know what, I can. We were using a Roland 808 drum machine as time keeper and rhythmic inspiration and I have a visual memory of turning that big tempo knob down and adding another kick drum to the pattern so it would go [sings (dotted) rhythm] and within a minute I landed on that famous guitar riff, that [plays famous guitar riff]. That was my big contribution to that recording. When I heard her sing that song with that guitar riff, I knew something was happening.

Getting back to the case in point, I knew when I heard Joan sing 'One Of Us' that the skies were going to open. I remember getting in my car with the cassette, just the guitar and vocal demo, I started working on the Grammy speech I should have gotten to give! The only time I had that feeling before was when I heard the first draft of 'Time After Time', which went on to be a hit for Cyndi Lauper. When I heard the first verse and chorus, I said 'congratulations, you've just written a hit'.

You mentioned the guitar riff you came up with for 'Girls Just Wanna Have Fun', which is one of that song's defining features. There are many examples of songs that have an instrumental signature of this sort. For instance, there's a song you wrote for Jon Bon Jovi's solo record called 'Ugly' in which there's a prominent pentatonic guitar riff. Do you sometimes begin to compose a song by coming up with a riff or motif like that?

I usually do. That's how 'One Of Us' was written. As it happens, 'Ugly' didn't come about that way, but, yes, my process tends to be that I get the riff first. In 'One Of Us', part of the time the vocal melody is parroting the guitar riff and the rest of the time it's filling in the holes around it. I've often wondered about U2 records because - at least in the good ones - the guitar tends to be playing a melodic part counter to the melody. And I often wonder which came first, the chicken or the egg.

Sometimes it happens that the lyrics come first and the lyrics strongly suggest a rhythm which in turn suggests a melody.

Yes. I have a friend who sent me a lyric which was intriguing and very clever and very touching at the same time, so I decided to give it a shot and I ended up writing one of the most challenging musical pieces I've ever done. I'm very proud of it. It's just amazing how a lyric is able to inspire a melody.

One of the purposes of this book is to raise people's awareness of key, of the vocabulary of chords and notes they use when they're writing in a particular key...

Like D minor, the saddest of all possible keys!

Exactly! When you begin to write a song do you think, 'okay, I'm starting off on a G major chord', at which point the vocabulary of chords and notes in the key of G major opens up in your head?

Oh, absolutely. And so much of it is dictated by the instrument. The 'One Of Us' riff on the guitar, if I wanted to do that in E♭ minor it would sound ridiculous. In fact, one of the reasons I came up with that mandolin riff is because I wanted to sing it in that key.

You mean that it would sound ridiculous because you wouldn't be able to utilise the open strings of the guitar?

Yes, and actually for the F♯ minor version we did with Joan I used a capo at the guitar. If I'm writing at the guitar and I start with a riff or a chord progression, I'll try it in different keys just to see whether it will work and whether it will inspire a vocal melody. Since a lot of the time that doesn't translate on the guitar well, I like to go back and forth between the guitar and the piano.

The instrument you're composing at can really define the way a song ends up sounding.

Absolutely. I rarely compose at the piano, it's almost always a guitar or a mandolin or mandola. I guess because those instruments are somewhat more limited. The geometry of the instrument will dictate what you play. But I actually like to work on the piano for melodies. My theory is that if you can't play a melody with one finger then it's not a good melody. A good vocal melody you really can play with one finger; if you need more than that, you don't have it right!

It's interesting watching the 'Idol' competitions where the singers aren't allowed to have an instrument, and you really hear what a song is made of when you hear it unaccompanied. A lot of so-called hit songs are kind of rubbish because - well, a great melody will suggest the chords. A lot of these songs that they sing, you don't get that.

They're just wandering, a collection of notes, and there's a difference between a collection of notes and a melody. A melody has an arc, a way of holding together, a way of informing the listener of the underlying harmonies. [Sings 'Somewhere Over The Rainbow'.] Even if you're not a musician you hear the chords. [Sings 'Hey Jude'.] It's all in there. It's the same thing with lyrics, a bunch of words strung together is not a lyric. Even great poetry isn't necessarily a lyric. A great cliché I use is that words aren't a lyric until they have a melody and a melody is not a melody until it has a lyric.

The melodies you just sang have a real balance to them, a balance between stepwise motion and jumps, and there is also a balance between where they ascend and where they descend. It's difficult to make a formula out of that, though, isn't it? It seems to work in those instances, but there are so many variables.

If there were a formula, we'd all be geniuses.

People have an instrument that is their main instrument, and they have these familiar chord patterns that they're used to playing when they begin to write a song, they get into these finger habits so everything they do ends up sounding samey. Do you have any advice for songwriters on how to get out of these ruts? You actually suggested one way they might get out of it earlier; by turning to a less familiar instrument.

Then when you come back to your original instrument, your instrument of choice and convenience, you'll find that you have new ideas on it. But yes, especially after 'One Of Us', which I wrote in my usual style, by picking bass notes with my pick and playing the melody with my third and fourth fingers, its success was a validation of that style and I wrote a lot of songs like that afterwards. But I'm constantly trying different approaches. Some people use altered tunings, that's one way of doing it. I've started listening to Hendrix again, that helps, and I've gone back to playing a Stratocaster rather than a Les Paul, and that completely changes my approach to the instrument.

The string spacing is different.

And the scale length. And having a whammy bar, all of a sudden I'm Jimi Hendrix, I'm Jeff Beck.

The most radical solution would be to do the whole classical composer thing and step away from an instrument completely and write quite a bit of a song in your head.

I keep meaning to do that! I hear that that's how Joe Jackson composes. He doesn't go to an instrument until he has the melody. I have worked with people who write completely melodically; even though they have access to an instrument they will sing melodies. My job is then to harmonize the melody they came up with.

Writing in your head can be problematic in the tradition of recorded music because things can easily become unidiomatic. If you're writing a dance track you really want to have access to a synth, if you're writing a blues song you don't really want to be away from the guitar.

Still, the thing that separates a good blues song from a mediocre blues song is a real melody. There's a reason blues bands have been doing 'Stormy Monday' since time immemorial; it's because it has a really good melody. Or 'Born Under A Bad Sign', there's a really good melody there. That melody transcends the genre. Even in dance music, most dance music is sort of [sings 'boom chik boom chik boom chik'] and then just a pentatonic melody. The reason Lady Gaga is huge is that she writes real melodies. I saw her sit at a piano and sing 'Paparazzi', and that's really what changed my mind about her. It opened my eyes to her, realising that she's a real songwriter, and it's very possible that she does write those songs in her head.

I think greatness comes from stepping out of the idiom. There are people who write in an idiom and they make a track that sounds like a hit and they find a melody that works for them... really, most of these people are hacks in my opinion. And I know a few of them. And I've seen them say, calculatingly, 'I'm going to make my own version of a song that's big on the radio right now.' After 'One Of Us' a number of songs came out that used the same 'sensitive female songwriter' chord progression, VI, IV, I, V.

Now, I didn't invent that chord progression. There have been examples of that progression prior to 'One Of Us', although not very many. There are loads of songs being played on the radio at the moment that use those chords. Sometimes it starts on the VI and goes to the IV and sometimes it starts in the middle, on the I, before progressing to the V, VI and IV. Think of the current hit by Iyaz, 'Replay'. I think the earliest use of it is Scott McKenzie, 'If You're Going To San Francisco'. A journalist I spoke to about the history of this chord progression says that he can't find any examples of it in classical music. I suppose that classical music isn't so much about chord progressions, about a repeating cadence of chords.

One of the good things about composing in your head is that it can force you to come up with melodies that are more simple than what you might come up with at an instrument. A melody can sound really good to you in your head and when you play it on the piano or guitar you realise how embarrassingly simple it is.

That's the elusive butterfly as a songwriter.

The other problem aspiring songwriters come up against is having written a chord progression, a section of music, they then run up against a wall where there doesn't seem to be anything obvious that goes with it. People get really stuck with that. Is this something you encounter less as you get older and your experience grows?

Absolutely not. I encounter it more. And I encounter it much more in collaborative situations. With two people working on a fragment, they're much more likely to stay on it, whereas when I'm working on my own I'll just try something else. Sometimes that original piece will resurface, the fragment will work in another setting.

That's perhaps the most elegant solution. When people start out songwriting I think they have a tendency to want to keep what they come up with at all costs. I think more experienced songwriters say, you know what, it's not working, I'm going to discard it and think about it again tomorrow.

Right. I catalogue everything, I have a folder on my desktop full of little audio clips of ideas I've had. Sometimes I go back and listen to them, but you know, things that I thought were so brilliant at the time usually don't suggest anything. I keep hoping they will, but they usually don't.

chapter five: common techniques

So FAR YOU HAVE PROBABLY been playing our four-bar chord progression by strumming it through with a relaxed right hand. There's absolutely nothing wrong with that, but for the purpose of songwriting at the guitar it is often a good idea to mix things up by playing chord progressions in different ways. Experimenting with some standard right- and left-hand techniques as you are composing will create new possibilities and allow you to take your songs into new territory.

picking

The articulation of individual notes within a chord is one of the most obvious alternatives to strumming. It is often effective to attack individual strings with your plectrum, bringing out interesting lines and melodies that are hiding in a chord progression. Jimi Hendrix's playing frequently applies inventive and ever-changing right-hand picking/strumming patterns to basic chords; consider 'Hey Joe', for example.

You don't need to be as good at off-the-cuff articulation as Jimi was, though. 'Street Spirit' by Radiohead, for example, applies a consistent picking pattern to a chord progression.

Taking 'Street Spirit' as our inspiration, let's apply a consistent picking pattern to our chord progression:

It sounds okay like this, but the progression could be further improved by creating a melodic line within the chords. Something like this:

A line has been created here by adding notes that were not originally part of the progression. There are plenty of possibilities when it comes to adding linear interest to the progression in this way. Here's another example:

Of course, the added notes change the harmony in these progressions, which is something you should be aware of. If a bass part or vocal melody for our progression were present we would need to be alert to the possibility of these added notes creating unwanted dissonance with these parts.

Sometimes the simplest solutions are the best, and there are ways of articulating individual notes in a chord that are more straightforward than the examples given above. The first two bars of REM's 'Everybody Hurts', for example, are harmonically simple, consisting of open Dmaj and Gmaj chords. No additional notes have been added to the basic major triads. Rather, each chord is played as a simple arpeggio. A large number of famous songs contain passages of basic major and minor chords played as arpeggios, such as 'Just Like A Woman' by Bob Dylan and 'Unchained Melody' by North/Zaret. Here is our familiar chord progression, arpeggiated:

fingerpicking

Fingerpicking is a staple technique of folk, indie and blues, and there are plenty of rock (Metallica's 'Nothing Else Matters') and pop (Fergie's 'Big Girls Don't Cry') songs that involve a fingerpicked guitar part.

For those unfamiliar with traditional fingerpicking, the important thing to remember is that the thumb operates the three low strings (E, A and D) while the index, middle and ring fingers operate the G, B and (thin) E strings respectively. Guitarists frequently deviate from this rule, usually in order to allow the index, middle and ring fingers to control the D, G and B strings when required. It is a good idea, however, for fingerpicking novices to stick to the rule stated above as much as possible.

It is common to employ an alternating-thumb picking pattern when fingerpicking. An alternating-thumb pattern involves the thumb picking either the E, A or D strings at regular intervals throughout every bar, typically once or twice every beat. Here is a normal alternating-thumb pattern on a Gmaj chord:

Make sure that every note you play has the same rhythmic value, as if following the tick of a metronome or clock. In keeping with the rule stated above, these notes should be played with your thumb only.

Once you are used to the pattern you can start to fill in the gaps with your remaining fingers.

Let's try the same thing with our four-bar progression, starting with the alternating thumb alone:

Now with the alternating thumb as part of a proper fingerpicking pattern:

In this adaptation of our progression, the Cmaj and Amin chords incorporate a low G and low E, the fifth of both triads respectively. It is idiomatic for an alternating thumb pattern to jump down to the low E string when the root of a chord is located on the A string. This means that any such chord will become a second inversion chord, if only momentarily.

The process of figuring out a fingerpicking pattern that will suit a particular chord progression is likely to give you new ideas. For example, some of the harmonic changes made to our progression in the previous chapter would fit in well with the alternating thumb pattern above.

There are other ways to approach fingerpicking a chord progression, of course. In the style of the hit ballad 'More Than Words' by Extreme, we could apply a different sort of picking pattern to our progression.

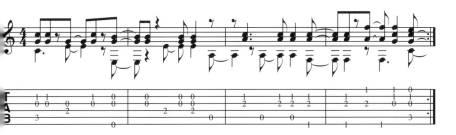

This is a less busy pattern altogether, one that would perhaps suit a simple, salient melody line. One advantage of this sort of picking pattern is that it is more likely to work on electric as well as acoustic guitar.

hammer-ons and pull-offs

As far as left-hand techniques go, there are only two worth mentioning; the hammer-on and the pull-off. If you have been playing the guitar for any length of time you will be familiar with these techniques, which involve the left hand generating notes without right-hand assistance. Hammer-ons and pull-offs (H&Ps) are not really associated with any genre in particular, although you would only expect to see a large number of consecutive H&Ps – sometimes known as left-hand legato playing – in an electric-guitar-driven rock or metal song.

When it comes to chord progressions, H&Ps are likely to be of ornamental value only. When it comes to riffs, however, it's a different story. Some of the greatest motifs in guitar history use H&Ps in abundance, from 'Layla' by Derek And The Dominos to 'Californication' by The Red Hot Chili Peppers.

chapter six:
composing lines

THE COMPOSITION OF A CHORD PROGRESSION is likely to occur when a songwriter is sitting at his instrument. One of the nice things about composing a motif, melody or bass line is that it can be sung – or hummed, or whistled – by the songwriter. In other words, linear material lends itself to being composed while you are away from your instrument.

composing in your head

The music you compose while showering or walking around the garden will have a different quality to music written at the guitar or piano, and there are a number of reasons for this. For one thing, your habits as an instrumentalist can easily come into play when you are composing at the guitar. Those familiar hand positions, chord shapes and habits can end up controlling the compositional process. In fact, the peculiar sensation of being an onlooker as your hands do the composing will be familiar to most guitarists!

Many of the great songwriters of the nineteenth century – composers such as Schubert and Brahms – would have felt comfortable with

the practice of writing an entire song without access to an instrument. Composing a modern-day pop or rock song in its entirety without an instrument, however, would probably be a bad idea. In order for a song to sound idiomatic, the conventions of the compositional process associated with the idiom in question need to be obeyed. Try writing a modern dance track without access to a computer, a blues song without access to a guitar, or a synth-pop song without access to a keyboard instrument of some sort. Unlike the tradition of classical music, in which there is a well-established process of composing without an instrument, all modern popular genres are associated closely with a method of songwriting that is very much instrument-dependent, whether that instrument is a guitar, a piano, or a piece of software such as Reason.

Composing an entire song in your head might be inadvisable, but composing memorable melodic or motivic material in your head is an excellent way to start writing a song. Begin by singing something to yourself absent-mindedly. Try not to evaluate the quality of what you're doing to begin with, just come up with something; quality control can come later.

To get yourself going you could try riffing on an interval, singing a major 3rd repeatedly, ascending and descending. Coupled with the right words, a simple interval can be evocative, and it can even become the signature of a piece of music. The ascending octave on the word 'somewhere' in 'Somewhere Over The Rainbow' from *The Wizard Of Oz* or the ascending major 7th on the words 'there's a…' in 'Somewhere' from *West Side Story* are instantly recognisable.

words

As you are singing your newly composed motif you will need to articulate words of some description, even if they are of the meaningless 'la-la-la' variety. If you are aiming to compose a vocal line specifically then you should aim to sing words – meaningful words – as you compose. The interplay between words and line in a sung melody is complex, and while there are plenty of precedents for inventing words and music separately, ideally there will be a point at which you come up with a melody or motif with words (or at least one word) attached.

In general, there is reason to be sceptical about the value of discussing the invention of lyrics and the process of combining lyrics with music. There are far too many variables in songwriting for there to be 'rules' with regard to lyrics. However, there is one maxim worth remembering; when writing a song you should be aware of the rhythm and emphasis of lyrics as they would occur in everyday speech. In other words, if you decide to set the sentence 'Why am I an elephant?' to music with a rest after the word 'am' and an emphasis on the second syllable of 'elephant', you should at least be aware that you are phrasing the sentence without regard to the rhythm and emphasis of everyday speech. (Needless to say, the first syllable in 'elephant' would be emphasised in everyday speech, while the word 'am' would be followed immediately by 'I'.)

Listen to some of your favourite songs, paying particular attention to the phrasing of the lyrics. How often do your favourite artists disregard the natural phrasing of a sentence by emphasising unexpected syllables and words? Unless your favourite artist is Captain Beefheart you will probably find that the phrasing of your favourite song lyrics is rarely incongruous with everyday speech.

the two-chord exercise

Many of us experience a feeling of uncertainty and even trepidation when we are required to invent something out of thin air. Music teachers the world over are familiar with the obvious unease students exhibit when asked to improvise or compose for the first time. When it comes to composition in particular, a significant proportion of music students are hesitant and unsure of themselves, sometimes so much so that they remain forever uncomfortable with the process of inventing music.

One of the inhibiting factors responsible for this phenomenon is surely the disparity between the typical newly-composed quantum of musical material and music as a finished article. Those of us who listen to recorded music will evaluate and attribute value to a song based on a plethora of factors, from the way it was structured, arranged, performed, mixed and mastered to the hairstyle of the lead singer in the music video. The hesitant music student is deprived of these aesthetic cues when composing a melody in isolation, for example. The four-bar motif he has just come up with... is it good? Is it awful? Without the multitude of factors to which his musical aesthetic has always related he is effectively lacking a musical aesthetic altogether. How can he continue to compose without any bearings? How can he decide which note or chord should come next?

At no point are you more likely to experience this sense of disorientation than when first attempting to compose away from your instrument. For this reason you may find it helpful to ease yourself into the process of composing in your head by trying to compose a vocal line while sitting with your guitar playing the most basic chord progression possible, one consisting of just two chords. Preferably these two chords should belong to the same key. Chords I and IV (Gmaj to Cmaj in the key of G major, for example) would be a typical choice, but any diatonic pairing will do.

Once you are comfortable with this two-chord exercise you should begin composing without recourse to the guitar. In general, try to get into the habit of humming or singing original material to yourself whenever possible. When you come up with a usable motif or melody you will need to do your best to remember it, at least until you can get back to your guitar or get hold of a pen and paper or a recording device.

The prospect of composing away from the guitar will be unattractive and completely unfamiliar to many readers. However, there is no shortage of music out there that should inspire you to try something new. There are many songwriters whose compositions benefit from their ability to 'think' music. Rivers Cuomo of Weezer is an excellent example of a songwriter who is able to invent strong, distinctly 'thought' melodies, even within the context of a heavily guitar-driven genre. In fact, Weezer's single 'Troublemaker' can be listened to as a model two-chord exercise.

chapter seven:
the applied
dominant revisited

We established earlier that the most common non-diatonic chord in modern songwriting is the applied dominant chord. In terms of music theory, the applied dominant chord is a relatively advanced concept, so it is worth revisiting.

The dominant chord in a given major or minor key is chord V, and the dominant relationship is chord V to chord I. An applied dominant chord applies the dominant relationship to chords other than chord V to chord I. This can only happen between chords that are commensurably spaced:

chord VI to chord II
chord VII to chord III
chord 'VIII' (that is, chord I) to chord IV
chord II to chord V
and chord III to chord VI

The applied dominant chord is the first chord in each of these pairings, the chord analogous to chord V in a normal dominant relationship of chord V to chord I.

In order to effect an applied dominant relationship it is not enough for you merely to play chord VI followed by chord II, for example. Chord VI needs to do its best impersonation of a dominant chord; it needs to become either a major chord or a straight (as opposed to maj7 or min7) 7 chord.

an example...

As luck would have it, our old four-bar chord progression offers us an opportunity to effect an applied dominant relationship.

Here is the progression again, a four-bar progression through chords I, III, VI and IV in the key of C major:

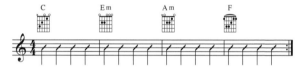

Four-bar progression

The relationship between chord III to chord VI (Emin to Amin) has the potential to become an applied dominant relationship. For chord III to become an applied dominant chord it needs to become a major chord or a 7 chord.

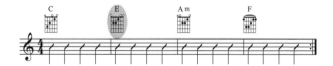

Of course, in some cases the chord we are treating as the applied dominant might be a major chord to begin with. The applied dominant relationship chord I to chord IV is a good example. Assuming we are in a major key, chord I will be a major chord. For the listener to understand that chord I is functioning as an applied dominant chord it is necessary to turn it into a straight 7 chord. Here is an example in C major:

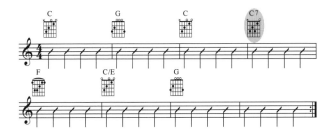

C7 is a non-diatonic chord in the key of C major; it contains a B♭, which is a diatonic note in the key of F major. The fact that it is followed by an Fmaj confirms that it is functioning as the applied dominant chord in a chord I to chord IV applied dominant relationship.

 The dominant seventh

Chord V7 (B7 in the key of E major, for example) is a chord that wears its dominant-ness with pride. Not only does it contain the (major) third that wants to resolve upwards to the tonic note, it has an added seventh that is the interval of a minor 7th above the root. This combination of a major third and a minor seventh is unique to the dominant seventh. Even out of context, a listener would be able to identify this chord as a sort of dominant chord, and from it he would be able to deduce the sound (if not the name) of the tonic chord for which it pines.

when to use an applied dominant chord

You should use an applied dominant chord when you suspect a chord progression is becoming predictable or bland. As with any non-diatonic chord, an applied dominant chord can add much-needed harmonic interest and piquancy to your song. In many cases, the substitution of a major chord for a minor chord (or a 7 chord for a major chord other than chord V) that shares the same root note is all that would be required to modify one of your existing progressions with an applied dominant chord.

Applied dominant variations

Any chord that is an extension of a dominant seventh (V7, a chord containing both major third and minor seventh) can function as an applied dominant chord. Chords such as a 7♭9 , 7♯9 (the 'Hendrix chord'), 9th, 11th and 13th are prime candidates. Certain added-note chords, such as add9 or add11, can also be used.

chapter eight:
modulation

You ARE NOW FAMILIAR with the idea of a piece of music being in a certain key. Generally, a modern-day pop or rock song will stay in one key for its duration, but some songs change key as they progress; they modulate.

For a song to modulate it needs to establish a new key. We have already seen that a vocabulary of diatonic chords and notes is established at the beginning of a song and that these notes and chords constitute a song's key. The key established at the beginning of a song is almost invariably what is known as the tonic key, the key in which a piece of music can be said to reside regardless of the many modulations that might occur as the piece progresses. It is traditional for a piece of music to end in the tonic key also, although this formality is not always observed in modern songwriting.

Establishing the tonic key at the beginning of a song is easy because the listener is ready and waiting to be introduced to a vocabulary of chords and notes that will constitute a song's key. Try picking up your guitar and slowly strumming an Emaj chord for a couple of bars. Even in the absence of other chords or a melody line, your brain will latch on to Emaj as the most likely tonic chord and you will even expect to hear chords in the key of E major following it up.

surprise tactics

Once the tonic key has been established, convincing the listener that a piece of music has moved to a new tonal centre is less straightforward. To launch into a new vocabulary of chords and notes is usually unsatisfactory unless you are aiming to surprise your audience! In the right context this can work well, though. The famous modulation on the word 'change' 2.52 minutes into 'Man In The Mirror' by Michael Jackson is a good example of an effective 'surprise!' key change. It works because we have already heard a similar build-up resolve to the word 'change' coinciding emphatically with the tonic chord, so we are susceptible to the idea that the word 'change' coincides with an affirmation of our home chord. Sure enough, the chord coinciding with the word 'change' at the 2.52-minute mark is the tonic chord, this time the tonic chord of a new key to which the song has modulated.

There are other reasons for the effectiveness of the sudden key-change in 'Man In The Mirror'. The one-beat rest before the change, for example, or the not-too-subtle symbolism of the word 'change' coinciding with, well, change. It is also significant that the key changes from G major to A♭ major.

Gear change

Abruptly modulating up a tone or semitone creates a sense of intensification, as though the music has shifted up a gear. Listen to Whitney Houston's rendition of 'I Will Always Love You', for example. This sort of modulation often appears near the end of a song, commencing at the start of a chorus.

key relationships

Music can be analysed in terms of harmonic strength; that is, how strongly the tonic chord or tonic note is affirmed by a chord progression or melody. A chord progression of particular harmonic strength might consist of prominent tonic and dominant chords, while a harmonically strong melody might tend to emphasise the notes of the tonic triad. Let us imagine the existence of a passage of music consisting of just such a chord progression and melody, and let us then imagine that it precedes a passage of music from which the tonic chord is absent and in which there are numerous inversion chords and the odd applied dominant chord. It would be fair to compare the two passages in terms of their harmonic strength, recognising the first passage as harmonically stronger – more affirmative of home – than the second.

A quote from page 15 of this very book: 'One could argue that the essence and complexity of music itself can be attributed to the relationship between notes and chords that are closer to home and notes and chords that are, to various degrees, further from home.' It would be unusual to encounter a piece of music containing successive passages of such contrasting harmonic strength as imagined in the previous paragraph. It often requires great skill on the part of the musical analyst to discern the varying degrees to which a piece of music leaves and returns to home as it progresses, home being the tonal centre whose ultimate affirmation comes in the form of the tonic chord in root position, set into relief by the dominant chord in root position. Fast-forward a recording of a classical symphony to its final bars and you will hear that these two chords (chord V to chord I, also known as a perfect cadence) are conclusive.

You should not infer from this discussion that harmonically stronger equals harmonically better. A song that does not contain a single perfect cadence – as indeed many songs do not – is not worse by any means than a song in which every phrase concludes with chord V followed by chord I. In order for a piece of music to be harmonically interesting it needs to do more than blandly affirm and reaffirm the tonic chord. Harmonic ambiguity, non-diatonic chords, the deliberate avoidance of the tonic chord in its root position, unexpected chord changes, dissonant chords; these are essential ingredients in an engaging, complex piece of music. As a songwriter it is up to you to decide where you want tension and ambiguity to reside in your work, whether you intend to take after The Magnetic Fields and Bob Dylan, combining straight, relatively predictable harmonies with ambiguous, attention-seeking lyrics; or whether you intend to take after Pink Floyd or Radiohead, generating drama and interest in your music with unconventional instrumentation and textures. Whatever your creative objectives, they will be served by your ability to control the inclusion or deliberate exclusion of harmonic interest, harmonic tension and harmonic ambiguity in your music.

With respect to modulation, the relationship between different keys can be compared to harmonic relationships (that is, relationships between chords within a key) in that keys can be more or less closely related to each other and, most importantly, more or less closely related to the tonic key of a song. We can gauge the proximity of one key to another by looking at how many diatonic chords they have in common. Let's use the key change from G major to A♭ major in 'Man In The Mirror' as an example.

G major contains the following diatonic chords:

Gmaj

Amin

Bmin

Cmaj

Dmaj

Emin

F♯dim

Here are the diatonic chords of A♭ major:

A♭ maj
B♭ min
Cmin
D♭ maj
E♭ maj
Fmin
Gdim

These keys do not have any diatonic chords in common. They are not closely related. This might come as a surprise since G major and A♭ major are separated by just one semitone, so they are closely related in terms of pitch. In fact, the proximity of two keys in terms of pitch does not correlate to how closely related they are in any meaningful sense as far as our current subject matter is concerned. Here is a circle of fifths, a diagram common to music theory textbooks:

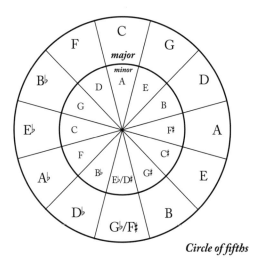

Circle of fifths

Each key is adjacent to its most closely related keys while more distantly related keys are progressively further away. Taking G major as our exemplar key again, we see that C major and D major are its neighbours. Let's take a look at the diatonic chords of these keys.

<u>*Gmaj*</u>	<u>*Cmaj*</u>	<u>*Dmaj*</u>
Gmaj	*Cmaj*	*Dmaj*
Amin	*Dmin*	*Emin*
Bmin	*Emin*	*F♯min*
Cmaj	*Fmaj*	*Gmaj*
Dmaj	*Gmaj*	*Amaj*
Emin	*Amin*	*Bmin*
F♯dim	*Bdim*	*C#dim*

Both D major and C major have four chords in common with G major, highlighted in red. On the other hand, D major and C major have two chords in common. This is as much as we would expect given that D major and C major are not neighbours in the circle, though they are relatively close together. G major and A♭ major are nowhere near each other, which is consistent with our observation that they have no diatonic chords in common.

In 'Man In The Mirror' there is a radical modulation between two keys that are only very distantly related. There can be no doubt that this is another reason for the effectiveness of the key change, which would be far less emphatic and startling were it to move between two closely related keys.

the relative minor/relative major

Every major key has a relative minor key with which it shares diatonic notes and chords. To state the obvious, every minor key has a relative major key with which it shares diatonic notes and chords. If the modulation in 'Man In The Mirror' had moved from G major to the relative minor key of E minor instead of from G major to A♭ major, the untrained listener would be less certain that a modulation had occurred at all, and the symbolism intended by the coincidence of the word 'change' with the modulation would be destroyed. Whatever key a piece of music is in, the relative minor/major key is the most closely related key.

The close relationship of a key to its relative minor/major key raises an interesting question: how is it possible to effect a key change between two keys that share an identical set of diatonic notes and chords? After all, the listener is usually alerted to a modulation by the introduction of notes that are not diatonic in the pre-modulation key.

Let's take a modulation from C major to its relative minor, A minor, as an example.

Here is the four-bar progression with the addition of a subsequent progression in A minor:

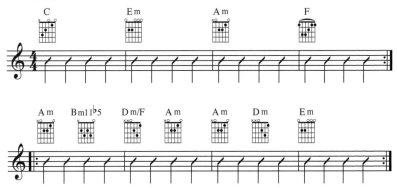

This example begins in C major and ends in A minor without introducing any notes that are not diatonic in C major. It succeeds in establishing the key of A minor in its second half by combining repetition of the new tonic chord (Amin) with the exclusion of those chords that would most strongly affirm C major, namely Cmaj, Gmaj and Fmaj (chords I, V and IV in the key of C major respectively).

When playing through this new progression, the more sharp-eared reader might notice that the final chord, Emin, doesn't sound quite right. This brings us to another method by which a relative minor key might be established: the sharpened leading note.

the leading note

'Leading note' is another term for the seventh degree of a major or minor scale. The leading note of C major would be B, for example, while the leading note of A minor would be G… or would it?!

In chapter one we saw that the dominant chord of a minor key is often a major chord, even though this would seem to include a non-diatonic note. In the key of A minor, this means we could use an Emaj chord rather than an Emin chord as our dominant chord. There is a one-note difference between these chords. The third of the triad is one semitone sharper in a major chord; the note G in Emin becomes G# in Emaj. When a majorised dominant chord is used in a minor key, the true leading note of our minor key – G# in this case – has been invoked.

The scale incorporating this leading note even has a name, the harmonic minor scale, which consists of the notes A, B, C, D, E, F and G# in the case of A minor. The viability of this scale has a significant bearing on the ease with which we will be able to modulate from a major key to its relative minor key – or vice versa – because we now have access to a note that is not diatonic in both keys. The listener will be alert to the possibility that a modulation is taking place as soon as he hears the introduction of the leading note of the relative minor key.

Here is the extended progression with the substitution of Emaj for Emin after the key change.

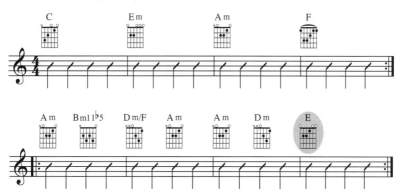

It should be noted that the sharpened leading note is most commonly used in the dominant chord of a minor key. Though no less viable, it is less usual for the sharpened leading note to be included in other diatonic chords such as chord III or chord VII.

just a minute...

We have just been discussing the means by which a modulation can be effected. Principally, this involves introducing notes that are not diatonic in the key from which the modulation is taking place. The dominant or dominant seventh chord of the key to which we are modulating is particularly effective in establishing this key.

With these facts in mind, you may well ask where applied dominant chords fit into all this. An applied dominant chord introduces a non-diatonic note in order to make a dominant-like relationship with a chord other than the tonic chord. Well, that sounds a lot like a modulation!

There are indeed ambiguous cases where it is difficult to identify a non-diatonic chord conclusively as being either an applied dominant chord or the dominant chord of a new key. This is a subjective area, and musicians sometimes speak about a new key being 'touched upon' where they do not feel it has been fully established. Generally, however, applied dominant chords function in much the same way as they do in the examples we've seen. They hint at a change of key fleetingly, perhaps, but fail to establish a new key for any significant length of time.

the pivot chord

A 'surprise!' modulation is relatively easy to achieve. We simply jump to a new key, alerting listeners to its arrival by using chords that were not diatonic in the preceding key. In order to transition smoothly from one key to another without startling the listener, however, we are in need of transitional chords that are common to both keys. These are known as pivot chords.

A smooth transition from C major to F major would require consideration of the diatonic chords common to both keys, namely Amin, Dmin, Cmaj and Fmaj. Rather than playing through an example at this point, coming up with your own modulation would be a worthwhile exercise. You could use our four-bar progression as your starting point before attempting a change of key to F major. By using pivot chords in conjunction with chords that are not diatonic in C major (such as Gmin, B♭maj and C7) you should be able to modulate. Changing key gracefully isn't easy, though, so don't expect to be successful straight away.

chapter nine:
the process itself

ONE OF THE OBVIOUS DIFFICULTIES associated with any enterprise conducted in solitude is that it cannot be observed. The habits and methods of songwriters at work are rarely discussed in interviews and articles in the mainstream music press, for such detail would be of little interest to the ordinary music fan. The interviews with established songwriters contained in these pages deal with working practices, but this is extraordinary, and generally the aspiring songwriter is left to refine her working practice in a state of insecurity, with no way of knowing whether she is going about things in the 'right' way.

To make another rather obvious point, it is – in addition to being a difficulty – a condition of fecundity that the songwriter is bound to refine her working practice in isolation. The arts practised in solitude such as the composition of poetry and music require an artist to develop her own systems, habits and processes in order that the final work of art might stand a chance of being truly hers, an expression above all of the mind that gave it birth.

When songwriters find that their way of working is not producing songs of the desired quality or quantity, the fact that they have refined this way of working in isolation is not the cause of their failure as such. It would be more accurate to attribute failure to the fact that their isolation has been imperfect, that they have not been able to burgeon their craft in a vacuum. Problems often stem from received ideas of musicianship and songwriting rather than bad habits generated by an engagement with the craft itself. Therefore, when we try to change our creative habits as songwriters we should not idealise a conventional apprenticeship in which the apprentice apes the creative habits of her master, which is an approach hostile to the culture and tradition of writing good music of whatever sort. We should instead aim to learn from the example of other songwriters where it will bring us closer to a way of working that is more sympathetic to the demands of the creative act itself, as opposed to the nebulous, glamourised notions of the creative act that often accompany our formative musical experiences.

the game looks easy

As an extreme example of these detrimental notions, let's imagine a teenager who goes to see a film, *Amadeus*, which is a fictional account of the eighteenth-century composer W. A. Mozart and his genius. The teenager is inspired to become a composer and begins to write music for the first time. She is happy to begin with, but becomes increasingly disillusioned as she struggles to turn the many musical ideas she has amassed into coherent, finished pieces of music. She has inferred from *Amadeus* that the process of developing a musical idea involves an extension of the quasi-heroic inspiration involved in the invention of the musical idea itself. She is puzzled and disheartened that her moments of inspiration are too fleeting to sustain an uninterrupted flow of creativity that culminates in a finished work of art.

It is not necessary for a songwriter to have seen *Amadeus* or something like it before she risks labouring under romantic misconceptions about the artistic process. In fact, mystification of the artistic process is so widespread that the quickest and easiest thing would be to identify the few books, lectures, films and conversations on the subject that have not sought to shroud it in mystery. We breathe in this moon dust long before we attempt to write our first song, and this is to say nothing of the glamour of polished, multitrack-recorded music that is usually behind our desire to write songs in the first place. Music is showbusiness, after all, and making things look easy is a requirement of showmanship!

The reader may well dismiss all these observations as being so obvious that they are unworthy of expression. It is hardly revelatory to state that the creative act involves tedious struggle with small details, discipline, the rejection of material that has absorbed considerable time and effort. Yet any experienced teacher of composition will be used to encountering students affected by a malady similar to that of our imaginary *Amadeus*-watching teenager; students in need of reassurance that, yes, the process of writing a piece of music is supposed to be *that* difficult. The fact that they are struggling does not mean they are doing something wrong, nor does it mean they lack ability. The interviews contained here should reinforce the idea that achieving success as a songwriter requires a serious commitment. It is, for example, not an activity to be practised only when the songwriter feels like it, and it involves a path littered with abandoned ideas and time that seems to have been wasted. This was true for great songwriters such as Schumann and Brahms, and it is true for you and me.

self-criticism

One could argue that the most talented songwriters are likely to be among those who experience the creative process as a struggle. The ability to criticise one's creations is a prerequisite of artistic development and an expedient of artistic success, and songwriters who recognise this will be in no hurry to be impressed by their own inventions. Perhaps the best definition of artistic talent is sensitivity to the disparity between a piece of art and a self-imposed artistic ideal, the difference between an artwork as it is and as it should be.

This is an aspect of self-criticism as it relates to the creative process, but there is another, contradictory aspect of self-criticism. It is common for artists and writers to depend on meditation, free association, the consumption of alcohol – anything that will numb or circumvent their self-critical faculties.

There can be a punitive dimension to self-criticism where the artist is primed to reprimand herself for the inadequacy of her ideas before ideas have even emerged. For this reason, many artists feel that nothing is more likely to inhibit invention than self-criticism. While there is no straightforward recipe for the conciliation of self-criticism's contradictory aspects, we can at least identify an unhelpful idea that perpetuates artists' fear of self-criticism. It is an idea lurking behind the 'self' in 'self-criticism'; it is the artist's notion that her artwork is really a representation of herself, something that stands or falls on its own terms in the way she – an individuated, self-defining human being – stands or falls on her own terms. When this idea reigns unopposed in the artist's imagination, the prospect of artistic failure becomes fearsome and the small failures that are an unavoidable part of the creative process begin to hurt more than they should, leading the artist to fear the self-criticism that reveals them.

The idea that art aspires to be an expression above all of the mind that gave it birth is in no sense illegitimate. The problem is that it is an idea presented in an unbalanced way by the innumerable sources of *Amadeus*-esque mystification to which the artist is exposed. There is an equally legitimate, equally important way of looking at art that is ritually ignored, an idea that is the natural counterweight to the idea of art as individuated, individualistic self-expression. The process of writing a song, for example, can be described as the reception of a gift from God, something transcendental: 'Where did it come from?' wonders the songwriter before she answers her own question, 'It is my hidden soul's true expression!' There is nothing wrong with evaluating the process of writing a song in these terms, but it should not obliterate another truth; that the process of writing a song is as much like filling out a form as it is like writing a journal; it is as accurate to describe it as an act of conformity as it is to describe it as an act of individuality; it rewards derivation as much as it rewards originality. When the artist is able to recognise that art as self-expression and art as mere formality are not the contradictory ideas they would first appear she is able to criticise her inventions with less trepidation in the knowledge that their success or failure depends on her ability to represent received ideas as much as her ability to represent her self.

self-limitation

In practical terms, the most effective way to improve the quality of your songwriting is to limit yourself. The two-chord progression advocated earlier is just one example of self-imposed limitation. As an exercise, some songwriters will give themselves a meagre twenty minutes to write an entire song from start to finish. Or they will limit the scope of a song by employing a restrictive form or device, such as a ground bass, in which a bass line lasting, say, ten bars is repeated continuously throughout a song.

It would be wrong to suggest specific self-limitations for songwriters here; thinking them up is half the fun. One of the interesting things about the famous Goethe quote, 'limitation shows the master', is that – in translation, anyway – it can be taken to mean two rather different things. It could mean that an artist's skills are most obvious when she is working within stringent limits. Or it could mean that the artist reveals herself as a 'master' merely by virtue of her decision to work within stringent limits. Goethe probably intended the former, but it is the second meaning that is most useful to a developing songwriter. Listen to the music of your favourite songwriters and consider the skill they exhibit, not through a choice of chord or word, but through their surrender to a confining formal, conceptual, harmonic, rhythmic or lyrical norm.

songwriter interview: stephin merritt

I wrote to the celebrated songwriter Stephin Merritt of The Magnetic Fields to ask him about his approach to songwriting. His responses seem to resonate with the ideas explored in the preceding chapter, so they are included here.

Can you describe your creative process?

My everyday writing routine is to go out to some comfortable neighbourhood gay bar, one quiet and relaxed enough to be occupied mostly by old men chatting and gossiping. I bring my pocket-size blank book (too expensive to lose, but too small for its loss to ruin me) and a pen that won't explode in my pocket, having learned and relearned that decent pens are cheaper than decent pants. I order a nursable drink – cognac, usually – and sit near a light source. For a few hours I listen vaguely to the music and eavesdrop, and write down any ideas that come to mind, which may have nothing directly to do with songwriting. If nothing of use arises, I will have spent a pleasant evening lost in thought, and had a few glasses of cognac.

When useful ideas arise, they may be musical (generally variations on what I am hearing), lyrical (ditto), conceptual ('what if atonal music became popular?'), or a title ('My Atonal Baby') and any of those may be the germ of a song idea.

To help me remember a purely melodic idea, I may jot down dummy lyrics so dumb I can't possibly mistake them for just a bad idea; but ordinarily the melodic and lyrical kernels develop together. I don't like to work with verse that isn't at least vaguely set to melody, because the prosody will be awkward and require difficult revisions later on. And conversely a melody without at least a dummy lyric is not something I will be likely to remember tomorrow.

This is why my melodies are catchy. Because I don't write at an instrument, I don't have the melody in my muscle memory the next day, so only the melodic contour itself lingers, divorced from instrument and key, and not specifically harmonized or associated with any particular beat or tempo. It's also why my chord progressions are boring; I really don't care about chord progressions. They don't get stuck in my head. I know plenty of folk and jazz songs that can be done perfectly well in major or minor versions – or waltzed or swung, for that matter – and be perfectly recognisable. One would have a hard time writing any of them on, say, a 12-string guitar. Writing on instruments (like practising) is for instrumentalists, not songwriters. I don't even arrange using an instrument.

Even for a songwriter with your experience, there must be occasions when you feel at a loss to add a subsequent section of music that goes with what you have already written. How do you overcome this problem?

Keep it short. I like short songs. Why does everything have to be four minutes long? Lesley Gore's 'Sunshine, Lollipops and Rainbows' is perfect at 1:37. 'Sodomy' from *Hair* completes its AAB form within its 55 little seconds. I'm five foot three, I have a Chihuahua, I drive a Mini, I live in a studio, I play the ukulele. I am comfortable with miniatures.

It sometimes seems as though you gravitate towards helpful restrictions, which not only apply to the form of individual songs, but to whole albums. **69 Love Songs** *by The Magnetic Fields could be seen as an extreme example of self-imposed creative restriction. What exactly do you gain by setting yourself clearly defined limitations?*

If you decide to write a whole album about *I Love Lucy*, it's not really a constraint, it's a (vast) source of material. But if you decided to write a whole album without once mentioning *I Love Lucy*, that would be a constraint, but not a creatively fruitful one, unless Lucy had been the focus of your previous ten records. So writing *69 Love Songs* was not a constraint, except that the song 'Meaningless', which dismisses ironically a failed love affair, has much of its meaning diminished by being labelled a love song, which gives the game away. I just didn't notice that until it was too late.

Are there any songs you have written that spring to mind as being particularly good examples of self-imposed limitation?

'Punk Love' is a favourite song that would be unlikely to exist outside of *69 Love Songs*. It reminds me of those Japanese ink paintings made with one flick of a very clunky brush.

Which songwriters do you regard as the best composers of melodies from whom to learn?

I look to Irving Berlin for simplicity (steps), Brian Wilson for soaring (leaps), and ABBA for both.

A trite question, maybe, but I have to ask: is there any advice you would give to someone hoping to make a career as a songwriter?

Work harder, so when success falls in your lap you won't feel guilty. And for lyric material combining depth and detachment, don't forget to have a horrible love life.

chapter ten: an examination of 'shining light'

WE ARE NOW EQUIPPED to examine a complete song in more detail. The song in this case is going to be the radio edit (4m:07s) of 'Shining Light' by Ash, a suitably well-known, guitaristic song. It has been covered by several artists, including Annie Lennox in 2009.

 Caution!

This is a highly technical chapter. Take your time over each paragraph of analysis, looking closely at the section of music to which it refers. You should pay attention to the staves of conventional notation as well as the tablature, following the shape and rhythm of the vocal melody as best you can, whether you are able to read music or not.

Here are the introductory four bars:

Intro

These bars establish the tonic key of 'Shining Light'. As it happens, this introduction also establishes the chord progression that will be used in the verse.

When you begin to examine or learn to play a song you should be certain of the tonic key and its diatonic notes and chords. In this case the first chord we hear is Dmaj, so the chances are that the tonic key of the song is D major. The diatonic notes of D major are D, E, F♯, G, A, B and C♯. The basic diatonic triads are:

> *Dmaj*
> *Emin*
> *F♯min*
> *Gmaj*
> *Amaj*
> *Bmin*
> *C♯dim*

The chords used to establish the tonic key in the introduction are Dmaj, Gmaj, Bmin and Dmaj/C♯, which are all diatonic in D major. Notice that the introduction begins and ends with a bar consisting of a Dmaj chord only. We can say with certainty that D major is the tonic key.

a word on key signatures

This book is determined as far as possible not to rely upon conventional notation. However, recognition of a song's key is so much easier when we are able to refer to the key signature.

The key signature can be found at the beginning of each stave. Take a look at the intro to 'Shining Light'. See those two ♯s right after the treble clef (𝄞)? That's the key signature. Those two sharps tell us that this piece is either in the key of D major or its relative minor, B minor. If we see three sharps at the beginning of a stave, for example, we know the piece is either in the key of A major or F♯ minor. If we see three flat signs, we know that we are in the key of E♭ major or C minor.

🎸 *Key signatures*

1♯ = G major / E minor	1♭ = F major / D minor
2♯s = D major / B minor	2♭s = B♭ major / G minor
3♯s = A major / F♯ minor	3♭s = E♭ major / C minor
4♯s = E major / C♯ minor	4♭s = A♭ major / F minor
5♯s = B major / G♯ minor	5♭s = D♭ major / B♭ minor
6♯s = F♯ major / D♯ minor	6♭s = G♭ major / E♭ minor
7♯s = C♯ major / A♯ minor	7♭s = C♭ major / A♭ minor
No ♯s or ♭s = C major / A minor	

Here are the first ten bars of the verse of 'Shining Light':

Verse 1

The first eight bars of the verse consist of two near-identical four-bar phrases. The notion of a musical phrase is difficult to describe with precision. Musicians sometimes disagree about exactly where one phrase ends and the next begins. In this case you should be able to tell that the first four bars of the verse are a complete phrase, lyrically and musically. Sing it through to yourself if in doubt!

Melodically, there are two two-bar motifs in each of these four-bar phrases. In the case of the first four-bar phrase of the first verse, the melodies associated with the words 'Roman candles that burn in the night...' and '...yeah, you are a shining light' are each comprised of a distinct two-bar motif.

After the first eight bars of the verse there are two bars that conclude the verse, repeating the chords associated with the '...yeah, you are a shining light' melodic motif. This time the vocal line changes course and concludes on a strong D, which is, of course, the tonic note.

So, the first verse is ten bars long, consisting of two four-bar phrases which in turn consist of two distinct melodic motifs. The final two bars of the first verse are a sort of afterthought of the preceding phrases, and they conclude strongly on the tonic chord of Dmaj.

How can I identify the key of a progression?

More often than not, the first chord of a progression will be the tonic chord.

If you are looking at sheet music, the key signature will give away the key.

If a progression is diatonic, you could catalogue the notes it uses and deduce its underlying scale and key accordingly. A word of warning though; if a song uses non-diatonic notes, you might find it tricky to work out which notes are diatonic and which are not!

The most final-sounding chord is the tonic chord. Find that, and you have your key.

Verse two is practically identical to verse one. The only remarkable differences are new lyrics and the introduction of an ebowed lead guitar line.

In order that our examination of 'Shining Light' might reveal the secrets of successful songwriting, we should look for its most salient and recognisable features. The two melodic motifs that constitute the verse's recurring four-bar phrase contain two features that characterise the verse. The first is the four notes (G, A, G, F♯) of the melody on the words 'burn in the night', which are anticipated by the guitar riff in the second bar of the introduction. These notes are a mainstay of the verse; even when there are three syllables rather than four in the concomitant lyrics (such as 'constant source' and 'infinite'), the four notes are accommodated.

The second stand-out feature is the upward jump from D to B on the syllables '[are] a shin-[ing light]'. D to B forms the melodic interval of a major 6th, which is a big leap in a verse melody line that generally moves in steps of tones or semitones. It is no accident that this interval announces the arrival of the titular lyric 'shining light'.

 Learn to soar

These observations might suggest something to you in terms of your own songwriting. You may be aware already, for example, that the melodic interval of an ascending major 6th – even though you might not have known it by name – is often particularly effective in the context of a vocal line or prominent melody. Our observations about the characteristic jump from D to B in the verse of 'Shining Light' seem to confirm this, and there are indeed numerous famous melodies and motifs whose memorability owes something to the presence of an ascending major 6th.

Similarly, observing the manner in which a succession of four notes (G, A, G, F♯) is accommodated by a variety of lyrics might provide you with better insight into the use of syllabic vocal lines in your own songs. A melody can be said to be syllabic when each syllable of the lyrics is carried by a single note, as they are during the words 'Roman candles that burn in the night...' at the beginning of the verse. Look again at the your own songs' vocal melodies. Are they entirely syllabic, or are there occasional syllables that are carried by more than one note, like the 'light' in 'shining light' in bars 3–4 of the verse of 'Shining Light', which is carried by two notes (B and A)? Perhaps your melodies contain melisma, in which a single syllable is carried by a number of notes, as Aretha Franklin or

> *Stevie Wonder might employ, or a showy* American Idol *wannabe might abuse? You may see fit to revise some of your existing songs, ensuring that melodies deviate from the syllabic norm only where there is lyrical or musical material deserving emphasis.*

structural terms

Terms such as verse, chorus and bridge are used to describe the distinct sections of a song. It's likely that you are familiar enough with these common terms to have understood this chapter so far. Still, it would be a good idea to have a proper definition to which we can refer, as far as a proper definition of such moot terms is possible.

One point upon which everyone can agree is the typical presence of verse and chorus. There they are in just about any song you could name, in any popular genre from folk to metal to rap. Exactly what is the difference between verse and chorus, though? We can only generalise, and there will be a horde of counterexamples ready to shoot down whatever generalisations we make.

In poetry there is such a thing as verse-and-refrain form, in which a verse (that is, a group of lines forming a unit of the poem) or series of verses are always followed by a recurring refrain. In verse-and-refrain form the words of the refrain will not vary, or will vary only slightly, while every verse will be different. In music, the words chorus and refrain are used interchangeably, and the archetypal verse-chorus-verse-chorus pattern is usually a lot like verse-and-refrain form; the verse lyrics will be different each time while the chorus will be the same each time. As we are about to see, the verse and chorus of 'Shining Light' follow this rule, as do the verses and choruses of the majority of well-known songs.

That takes care of the lyrics, but the musical differences between verse and chorus are harder to pin down. There will often be a change in harmonic rhythm in the chorus; at some point during the chorus the rate at which chords change will either increase or decrease compared to the rate at which chords change during the verse or bridge. We might also expect to find a more rhapsodic, soaring melody line in a chorus, while in a verse it would be usual to find a more syllabic melody sung in a slightly lower register with shorter notes overall. Please remember that these are reckless generalisations, though.

Some songs have more than one type of chorus, a chorus A and a chorus B. Sometimes a song will have a 'double chorus' where the chorus has two distinct sections.

Of the other terms used to describe the various sections of a song, intro, solo and outro (or coda) do not require an explanation here. These sections may or may not feature material from the verse or chorus of a song, but they are usually fairly easy to recognise as distinct sections in their own right. The terms bridge, pre-chorus and middle-eight, however, can be confusing because of inconsistencies between English and American usage.

 What is a phrase?

A phrase is the musical equivalent of a line of verse, or a sentence of speech. Voices, wind instruments and strings can only produce a limited number of notes in succession before they exhaust breath or bow. This technical limitation is integral to the tradition of western music; therefore, the idea of the phrase is integral to the tradition of western music.

Sometimes the verse of a song will seem to have two distinct sections. It is unusual to see these marked 'verse A' and 'verse B', however, because the second section of the verse – the section that presumably comes right before the chorus – is called the bridge. You can think of the bridge as a distinct section of music that links verse and chorus, though it should be remembered that a huge number of songs do not contain such a section. If you live in America, the correct term for this section is pre-chorus, not bridge.

The term middle-eight is used to describe a section of new material typically lasting eight bars that occurs around or after the midway point of a song. There is usually a vocal part in a middle-eight with a degree of importance similar to the vocal parts of the preceding verses and choruses. If a song has an instrumental solo, it is likely to be immediately preceded or followed by a middle-eight. If you live in America, the correct term for this section is bridge, not middle-eight!

So, the term bridge refers to two completely different sections depending on whether you are using English or American terminology. This book will stick to the English convention of using the term bridge to refer to a section of music linking verse and chorus.

The introduction and verses of 'Shining Light' we have examined are followed directly by the chorus. Here is the chorus in full:

Chorus

The harmonic vocabulary of the chorus is similar to that of the verse. As in the verse, these chords are entirely diatonic and there is never any doubt that Dmaj is the tonic chord.

Harmonically, there are two features that distinguish the verse and chorus of 'Shining Light':

1. The harmonic rhythm is slower and more predictable in the chorus than it is in the verse. There is one chord per bar in the chorus, while there are variously one, two or three chords per bar in the verse.

> *2. The dominant chord (chord V, which is Amaj in this case) is not present in the verse. By contrast, it is prominent in the chorus in that it is set up by an Asus4 chord in the chorus's seventh bar.*

It is common for a chorus to have a faster or slower harmonic rhythm than the verse (or bridge) that preceded it. As a songwriter, it is vital that you are conscious of changing harmonic rhythm when you evaluate a song, and you should look to include a change of harmonic rhythm between sections in your own songs. If the verse and chorus in one of your songs share the same harmonic rhythm and you don't want to change them, you could consider adding a bridge in which chords change at a different rate.

As for the absence of the dominant chord in the verse, this too is not uncommon. Bearing in mind that the dominant chord provides the greatest possible harmonic tension in relation to the tonic, it might be anticlimactic to have a strong dominant-tonic relationship in a song's early stages. A strong dominant chord at the end of a chorus before a return to tonic-centric verse material is more typical, and that's exactly what we have in 'Shining Light'.

chorus melody

The important characteristics of the vocal melody in the chorus of 'Shining Light' are quite different from those of the verse. For example, the central note of the verse's vocal line is the F♯ above middle C, while the central note of the chorus melody is higher, the A above middle C. Rhythmically, compare the opening notes of the chorus ('We made a connection...') with the opening of the verse. There is a 'patter' to the verse, a rhythm dictated by the lyrics. The chorus melody uses longer notes in general; the rhythm of the chorus melody does not take its cue from the rhythm of the lyrics in the same way.

One of the most distinctive moments in the chorus first appears on the words 'chemical reaction'. The syllable '-cal' in the third bar of the chorus is carried by two notes, the E above the C above middle C and the F♯ above middle C. The E is the highest note we have seen in the vocal line of the song so far. These two notes are a minor 7th apart, forming the largest melodic interval of the song, and a big leap by the standards of any vocal line.

Where should I place the highest and lowest notes in my melody?

It is good practice to watch out for extremes in a vocal melody such as the lowest note, the highest note and the largest melodic interval, especially when it comes to your own compositions. It is important that you are able to introduce these extremes at just the right point in your song. In fact, you might find it helpful to think of composition as a form of rhetoric akin to poetry or oratory when it comes to considerations such as emphasis, intensification, repetition and predictability. Consider the difference it would make to 'Shining Light' as a whole if the first verse were to begin with a soaring vocal line containing large melodic intervals while every subsequent verse featured a relatively static vocal melody. In this regard the song could then be compared to a speech or poem in which exciting text is blurted out at the beginning in an effort to grab an audience's attention.

The placement of extreme and salient features will to a large extent define the effectiveness of a piece of music. 'Features' is a vague word; here it is meant to include a great number of things, from the highest and lowest notes of a melody to sudden changes in instrumentation, harmonic rhythm and key. Every aspect of your song – harmony, rhythm, structure, melody, lyrics, instrumentation and production – will establish its own set of norms from which various degrees of deviation are possible.

Let us take key as an example. A key is established at the beginning of a song. The composer may choose to adhere to this norm by remaining in the same key throughout a song, or he may choose to deviate by changing key. Exactly when this deviation takes place during a song is of great importance, as is the extremeness of the deviation. A subtle modulation to a closely related key early in a song is one thing, while a sudden modulation to a distantly related key in the final chorus is quite another.

When you begin to compose a piece of music you are in the business of establishing norms. You must grasp that you are the person in charge of what these norms are! When the middle-eight of 'Shining Light' introduces a descending chromatic melody line over a static bass line, this is a deviation from a norm that was established earlier in the song. By contrast, your next composition might include a descending chromatic melody over a static bass line during its verse and chorus, and under these conditions a middle-eight like the one from 'Shining Light' would be a continuation of – as opposed to a deviation from – the norm.

beware the Norms of genre!

While there are internal, self-contained norms over which the composer has complete control in each song, there are also generic Norms, norms with a capital 'n'! These capital-n Norms are the conventions of genre. Let's pretend that the imaginary song from the previous paragraph were presented to the listener as a traditional blues song. The song would succeed in establishing a chromatic melody as a norm with a small 'n', but it would deviate from the Norm in that one would not expect a traditional blues song to feature a chromatic melody. By way of example, it would deviate from the Norm still further if it were presented to the listener as a piece of eighteenth-century classical music.

Just as the degree of adherence to and deviation from 'user defined' norms is a subtle, complex art form, the degree of adherence to and deviation from genre-specific Norms is a minefield of connotation through which the composer must navigate a safe (or deliberately

 *norms/Norms*

Norms and norms; are these terms used in this way elsewhere? No. The norms/Norms paradigm is unique to this book. The word 'norm' has been commandeered in the hope that it will aid the reader's understanding of an aspect of music that lacks an established nomenclature.

explosive) path. The greatest composers are those capable of the highest degree of skill and intelligence in referencing both the rhetorical, intrinsic norms of their music and the Norms of musical style and genre. Superlatives are rightfully reserved for a small group of 'serious' composers such as Bach, Beethoven and Zappa, but there are celebrated popular songwriters distinguished from their peers by their ability to write and perform music that is highly 'Norm-aware', or music that references the Norms of more than one genre. Think of the later albums of The Beatles, which reference the Norms of early American rock and roll, rhythm and blues, classical music and psychedelic rock. The iconic album *Nevermind* by Nirvana is a good example of an album that stood apart from other records of the time thanks to an ingenious synthesis of styles, referencing the Norms of hardcore punk, noise rock and mainstream pop.

Back to the music. The chorus is followed by a return to the verse. This time around there is only one instance of the verse. It is typical for there to be two successive verses at the beginning of a song, but for there to be one verse at a time thereafter, especially in mainstream pop music. It is interesting to note that the original album edit of 'Shining Light' contained a fourth instance of the verse at this point, but it was removed for the radio edit, probably with the intention of increasing the commercial viability of the song.

 More about norms/Norms

Examples are provided in this chapter with the intention of helping the reader to understand the concept of both norms and Norms. It should be understood, however, that references to, deviations from and inter-relationships between norms and Norms are often so subtle that they resist analysis in anything other than highly esoteric language – that is, if they are able to be written about at all! References to genre-specific Norms, for instance, can rarely be described in terms such as 'Oh! That section works because it sounds a bit like a blues song!'. The posture adopted by a piece of music in relation to the conventions of genre can rarely be described clearly and distinctly.

A reprise of the chorus follows, which is in turn followed by the middle-eight:

Middle-eight

Unlike the verse and chorus, which are centred on the tonic Dmaj chord, the middle-eight centres on the chord of Bmin for its first four bars. Again, it is typical for a middle-eight to emphasise the relative minor chord and/or key – B minor in this case – which is exactly what is happening here. Even the chromatically descending vocal line is typical of a middle-eight in that it offers a brief break from norms established by the song hitherto, providing the first and only non-diatonic notes of the song.

The middle-eight is followed by a guitar solo over the chord progression of the chorus.

So far the structure of 'Shining Light' has been that of the archetypal pop song, right up to the eight-bar middle-eight and the guitar solo over chorus harmonies. We might expect the song to conclude with a final reprise of the chorus, and this is exactly what happens.

Final chorus

There is a twist, though. The final chorus is in the key of E♭ major. This is precisely the sort of sudden key change intended to give the listener a sense that the music has moved up a gear, as discussed in the chapter on modulation. I will leave it to the reader to decide whether this particular modulation is effective, although it is worth noting that Annie Lennox did not think it necessary to include the key change in her excellent cover of 'Shining Light', which is worth listening to if only to compare it with the original album edit of 'Shining Light' as well as the radio edit examined here.

songwriter interview: tim wheeler

Tim Wheeler is the singer, guitarist and main songwriter in Ash, a Northern Irish rock group that has enjoyed worldwide success since the platinum-selling album 1977 *was released in 1996. Top-ten hits, platinum albums, critical acclaim and sold-out arenas have followed. As a songwriter, Wheeler is famous for marrying the influence of rock genres such as metal, grunge and indie rock to a strong pop sensibility. 'Goldfinger', 'Girl From Mars', 'Burn Baby Burn', 'Sometimes' and 'Shining Light' are just some of the anthemic Ash songs with which he his credited.*

You're touring at the moment. Do you get the chance to write songs while you're touring, or is it too hectic?

It's just impossible to concentrate when you're on tour, not enough to actually sit down and work on something. There are always too many breaks, too many things to do during the day for me to get a chance. I'll sometimes come up with little fragments, and I'll be able to work on them after the tour when I get back home. But in general, I think you need to be grounded to write songs.

One of the reasons for releasing twenty-six singles over the course of a year instead of recording a conventional album is that I wanted to see what it would be like to have an extended period for writing songs. Whenever we did an album it felt as though we were getting into the flow of it by the very end, that the channels were totally open by that point. It's easy to write songs when you're in practice. I'd find that I'd finish an album, and then I'd feel really sad because I knew we'd be going on tour for a year and a half and I wouldn't be able to properly write for a long time.

Sometimes songwriters take inspiration from things that happens to them while on tour.

I'm a different kind of writer, I'm not an observational writer. So maybe someone like Alex from the Arctic Monkeys, he probably gets great little stories and stuff. But my writing is more about feelings; I'm expressing different things.

Is it easier for you to write a whole load of songs in one go, then? Do you sort of take yourself away from it all and...?

Yes. We have a recording studio in New York and that has given us great freedom. I find the best way for me to write is to wait until I have the house to myself in the evenings. I just chill out at home, order in food, sit down and write a song. I search for melodies first; I try to get a good melody and occasionally I'll have a snippet of a lyric that will inspire a song, or sometimes a little lyrical idea will come out while I'm writing a melody. Most of the time I'll come to the song after it's all arranged and then write all the lyrics.

Isn't it harder to do it that way around?

Yes because you're out of the headspace you were in while you were writing it. The ultimate thing is to write the lyrics when you've just got the music and you're excited about it. But I burn out in concentration, it gets too intense. There's a limit I get to where I just have to step away from it for a while.

It's so easy – especially if you're writing in the studio – to get carried away with the recording and production side of things.

Yeah. And sometimes we do so many songs at once! Our drummer, Rick, lives in Scotland so he comes over and stays at my place for a few weeks while we develop the songs and normally by the time he leaves we're left with a batch of about eight songs. So I'm multitasking a lot which can be a little tricky. He came over once and we did twenty songs and then I had twenty sets of lyrics to write! It took a few months.

When Rick came over and you laid down those twenty lyric-less songs, how long did that take?

About three weeks. We arrange the songs and kick them into shape as a group.

That's a pretty good rate of songwriting. It works out as more than one song per day.

I'll normally have the verse and chorus, the melodies of a song all ready, the basic structure ready, then we flesh it out as a band. We decide if we want a guitar solo or a middle-eight and how we want to structure it, then I'll go off into the next room and come up with something. We'll normally kick a few songs into shape in one day. Rick's really fast, he'll usually record the drum tracks to three songs in a day. We've become quite efficient, we're a little bit factory-like.

So how many songs do you take through to completion on your own before you approach the band with them?

None. I guess that's the great thing about being in a band. I like collaboration, I like to allow room for spontaneous things to happen once we're playing as a group. I guess that gives it our sound, really. I never have any lyrics, I just mumble random things! I work in the same way when I'm writing songs on the guitar, trying out different chord progressions and singing gibberish. When Ash started, some friends of ours had a band and the singer never wrote lyrics. He would just go and do gigs and sing whatever words came into his head over these set melodies. I was trying to emulate that when I first started writing. Also, I loved Nirvana, and it was hard to make out what Kurt was singing! I often listen to the recordings of me singing gibberish and find things that sound like words, and then the thing that sounds like a word will spark off a lyric.

So, the way I write is sitting down playing guitar chords and vocalising at the same time. I'm not singing any real words, I'm just sort of... singing. That's the way I find my melodies, with my voice. When I'm writing them in my voice, the melody and the key of the song will suit my voice automatically.

Every now and then I will get an isolated lyric first. Some of my best songs have been sparked off by a lyric, by a title. 'Girl From Mars', I had the title and thought I'm going to write a song. The title inspired me, and I was excited to come up with a piece of music. 'Shining Light' as well. The line 'you are a shining light' just popped into my head and I went home that night and I wrote it.

Did the melody to which those particular lyrics are sung come to you at the same time as the lyrics?

It was that evening. I had a girlfriend in Dublin and I was staying in my folks' place in Northern Ireland. I was staying there for a few months trying to write songs. I used to drive down to see her, spend time with her - I guess I would explain it as falling in love - and one day I just thought that about her, that lyric ['you are a shining light'] came into my head and I thought, that would be a good song. I was trying to be very disciplined, so I drove home to Northern Ireland that evening, a two-hour drive. I got home, got the guitar and was searching around for something. I think I was actually playing a riff from one of our other songs called 'Fortune Teller', which is a dirty sort of rock song. Out of messing around with that came the first three chords of 'Shining Light'. I guess that's when I came up with the refrain on the words 'you are a shining light'. Sometimes you come up with a phrase that you know will sing well rhythmically, you can derive the rhythm of the melody from the lyric.

In so many ways, 'Shining Light' is an archetypal pop song.

It's all diatonic!

Yes! Apart from the middle-eight which is in B minor. Even that is sort of archetypal, to have a diatonic piece in a major key that has a more chromatic middle-eight in the relative minor. Also, the way the vocal melody has a patter in the verse and then in the chorus –

It soars up.

Exactly.

It's got a middle-eight, it's got a guitar solo, it's got a lot of repetition in the verses, recurring phrases. Then it does have a key change. Some people are like, oh, the key change is a bit cheesy. The truck driver's gear change! It seems to grate with people sometimes, that sort of thing, but I like it. When we play it live, that's the moment people put their hands in the air; that has to be a good thing. We've got a song called 'Candy' that modulates up in a similar way.

We did an edit of 'Shining Light' for the single. We had to chop out half of the second verse and half of the middle-eight. In the old days we'd play the single version live, but the fans would complain to me! Radio expects a song to be under four minutes, so sometimes you have to make these sacrifices. So long as you aren't losing something important to the narrative of the song. It's always sad when you have to chuck away a couple of lines that you've slaved over. There have been times when we experiment with edits and we prefer them, they flow better. Chop bits out, get brutal and see how it goes. It's quite easy to do with computer editing, not like it was in the past.

Does the rest of the band have any input on the lyrics?

No, not at all. They've never really shown any interest. One time I was stuck on a song and I asked Rick for help, if he could sit down with me and we could write together. But in the end he probably only contributed two lines. I used to find lyrics a real struggle, the discipline of writing them. Melodies are sort of effortless for me, that's the one thing in my life that's easy for me. Writing lyrics takes so much more concentration, it's a different kind of thing.

When songwriters are asked, 'what's harder, music or lyrics?', the answer never seems to be 'music'. It can be really hard fitting lyrics to music, getting something that sounds right.

It's really tricky. I guess that's why in the old days it used to work so well to have the music writer and the lyricist.

Have you ever written music for someone else's lyrics?

Never. It would be an interesting experiment. That's what Brian Wilson did with *Pet Sounds*, found someone else to write the lyrics. I did once set a poem to music, a thirteenth-century Irish poem called 'Thou Shall Not Die'. I read it and thought, this sounds like a song, let's put music to it. It was easy! I think 'Golden Slumbers' by The Beatles was written in that way. Paul McCartney was sitting at the piano at his sister's house and there was an old song called 'Golden Slumbers' in a song book sitting in front of him. He couldn't read music then, so he just made up his own music to the words.

Your lyrics in general contain quite a lot of pop-culture references. You have a recognisable, clearly defined lyrical style. Do you ever find that limiting, do you ever think that you'd like to try something different but fear losing your audience?

I'm not too concerned about that. I probably don't realise how much people do actually analyse the lyrics. Perhaps because they're quite personal, no one else in the band really talks to me about my lyrics. Not many people I work with actually discuss them. All I worry about is that I'm happy with them. It's been a long time since we actually had a producer who would sit down and say, oh that line needs revising, or now you've got to go and rewrite this whole thing. That's the sort of thing that would happen with our old producer Owen Morris, who would look at the lyrics and give us advice. It's probably been over ten years since anyone discussed my lyrics with me. I just work on them in my own way and hope that they're good! I don't worry too much about style, it's more about trying to express what I'm thinking.

I have a therapist in New York and the day after I see him is my favourite day for writing lyrics. I'm tapped into my subconscious, and I guess that's what being creative really is. Often songs will tell you stuff about yourself that is in your subconscious, stuff you're not really aware of, and then months later you'll look back and realise you were trying to tell yourself something. Lyrics can really say a lot about your life. If a song is a true expression of a personal feeling then it resonates much more. It's what people recognise and what appeals to people, I think, because it reflects something in them. People can tell if something's real. And I think you put more into a song if you're saying something about yourself.

Still, I love rhymes. Sometimes I'll try to write in non-rhyme. But I find now that I'm totally addicted to it and I can't help but write that way.

Do you have a rhyming dictionary?

That was one of my worst mistakes! Working on one of our records, *Meltdown*, I had a rhyming dictionary and it was terrible. I was under a lot of pressure to write the songs fast for that album. The rhyming dictionary sped everything up. I think those are some of my worst, cheesiest, least personal lyrics because of that. If you have a rhyming dictionary it's someone else putting ideas in your head rather than you finding what you really want to say. Sometimes I will look up rhymes online if I'm really stuck, going crazy in the studio. But it's something to be used sparingly.

Because you were successful so young, are there any songs you look back on and go, 'hmmm, I wouldn't do that now'?

Not too much. There are definitely some embarrassing ones, but my first single was 'Jack Names The Planets' which I wrote when I was fifteen. We still play it now, and 'Girl From Mars', one of our most recognised songs, I wrote when I was sixteen. They have a naive charm, and I don't think I'd be able to write a song like them now. I've moved on in so many ways, it's something I couldn't really tap into. There's a simplicity there that I suppose I find sometimes nowadays, but... I'm technically a better songwriter these days. Songwriting's all about finding the moments that are 'real', you'll get a few blinding songs in a year, maybe ten at most that really resonate. So it doesn't matter if I'm thirty-three or sixteen, I was lucky enough to be able to grab a couple of those when I was that young. The best way is to be in practice all the time, to write all the time, because you never know when it's going to come to you. You can't force it.

Is it really important to you to write regularly, then?

Yes, write regularly, because then there's less pressure on you. Otherwise, if you're sitting there with the pressure on that you have to write a great song, it's not going to happen. It's all about finding something that has a real feeling to it.

Do you try to write whether you feel like it or not, come what may?

Yes. It's always fun for me just sitting down to write, it's really meditative. It's relaxing, and I just don't worry if it's good or not. Even if it's crap, I'll just write something. I'll spend a few weeks trying to do that as often as possible. Then I'll go back three weeks later and listen back to everything I've done. It almost goes out of my head a lot of the time once I've written it, it's often just the first scrap of an idea, then I'll go back and see what there is and I'll find a few things that excite me. I'll then work on those and try to develop them further.

Quite a lot of material does get discarded, then.

Yeah, loads and loads. I probably write hundreds of songs - what could become hundreds of songs, but they're just fragments. It's a bit like sketching, I think. I just try to have fun doodling and see what happens.

I think that's a good attitude. People can get frustrated trying to perfect things all the time and running up against that brick wall.

It's a horrible feeling, and I've been there. I've had so much pressure on me to deliver follow-ups to things that I've ended up with writer's block. It's the most horrible thing. And forcing yourself to write songs, you're not going to get your best material that way. It's a mind game you have to play with yourself to take the pressure off yourself and just... enjoy it, really.

It's easy to run into the brick wall when trying to find a section of music that really complements what you already have.

Sometimes you'll come up with a chorus that you really like and no matter how hard you try you can't come up with a verse for it. I've got a chorus I've had since I was fifteen! I only realised last year that I had a verse that had been kicking around for a few years, one was a chorus looking for a verse, the other was a verse looking for a chorus. I realised one day that these two finally go together! It became a song called 'Gallows Hill', that was a bonus track, and our fans really love it. It's an interesting marriage of an old-school Ash chorus and a more up-to-date verse. It took fifteen years to find the right verse for that chorus! It shows that you can't force things. Eventually, some things will make sense.

Songwriters can be hindered by habits acquired at the guitar. One way of breaking these habits is to put down the guitar, take a walk and try to come up with a melody away from the instrument.

Yeah, I had a great one recently, one of the most popular of our new songs is a song called 'Arcadia'. It's got quite a distinctive melody that just popped in my head one day as I was walking into a studio. It just kept going round and round my head. I sat down at the piano and figured it out, it turned out to be a real killer, a real gift.

Often the stuff you come up with in your head is more simple than what you would come up with if you were at an instrument.

Definitely. If you write something in your head it's often just based around three simple chords. You're right, breaking habits is good because I've discovered writing using the computer in the last couple of years. I'll start with a drum beat and then start messing around with keyboards. I tend to write things that I wouldn't write on the guitar, I use chord progressions that I wouldn't use on the guitar. I'd think on the guitar, oh I've done that before too many times, I wouldn't do that again, but it feels fresh when you approach it on a different instrument. I think John Lennon turned to the piano later on with The Beatles because it was something he was unfamiliar with.

Even sometimes buying a new guitar that feels different! It has a different feel to it so you write something different. Or if you have a new guitar effect it will inspire a riff.

Do you have any other techniques for habit-breaking? Will you sometimes put your guitar into unfamiliar tunings?

Yes, that's the other one. Also, sometimes I'll use a capo, which can change the sort of melodies you'll come up with.

Is there a particular key towards which you gravitate?

I will write all over the neck of the guitar. I'm quite a rudimentary keyboard player, so a lot of our keyboard stuff is in C major. The old classic! They say Irving Berlin could only write in one key. He had one of those pianos where you could change key using a lever! It took me a while before I realised I could transpose something to make it easier for me to sing. As the years have gone on my range has gone higher and I try to push myself to sing in different registers.

Around the time Ash were starting, bands like Nirvana and The Pixies were huge, and those bands used a lot of power chords. With power chords you can move anywhere, you're quite free. Maybe that's why my keys are all over the place.

When you begin to write a song in a particular key, are you aware of the vocabulary of diatonic chords you are likely to use?

I have learned over the years where I can go in a certain key. It took me a long time to figure that out, and already by that time I'd written a lot of songs that were quite adventurous harmonically. It's about trying to be instinctive, and sitting down at the guitar trying to find something new. When I sit down I start fumbling around with chords, and then I will figure out the chords that go nicely, but I do tend to like finding those unusual jumps. I like to find chords that will pull us out of the key for a second and still fit with the melody. It's quite sneaky, deceptive; so people don't realise you're doing anything unusual.

That's a real feature of Ash's music. You certainly do that more than the average rock band.

Someone like Paul McCartney did it loads.

And Nirvana, they used lots of non-diatonic chords.

Yeah, I'd love to read an analysis of the songs of Nirvana. That's why I loved them, some of their harmonies sounded so exotic. They were a huge influence on Ash. We saw them play. It was very powerful, simple in some ways, but not melodically simple. I think people don't realise how sophisticated they were. Kurt Cobain had real songwriting talent. I think because they were a heavy three-piece rock group people didn't realise the melodic sophistication.

You have a strong pop sensibility as a writer. So who are your big influences?

When I was a kid it was The Beatles, so Lennon/McCartney. And George Harrison, too. One of the few decent records in my parents' record collection was this Beatles 'Oldies but Goldies' compilation. It was all really upbeat, early Beatles like 'I Want To Hold Your Hand' - these melodic, fast tunes. Then I got into metal as I got older, Megadeth and Iron Maiden. Then I got into the whole alt rock scene, Nirvana, The Pixies, Teenage Fanclub. I'm also into Brian Wilson, I love really melodic stuff. There's something I love about a melody that grabs you, that you can really get lost in. It's just pure pleasure, I don't want the music to be difficult or hard work. I love Abba as well! I like pop tunes that really stand up by themselves for three minutes, that are really self-contained.

I suppose having that pop sensibility comes with its own set of problems, especially when record companies want you to continually do 'the same again' because of your previous songs' popularity.

The first time I tried to write a song I'd had my first guitar for a few weeks and my Granny had died around that time; I was trying to express something about the way I felt at that time, and maybe that's why music and feelings are linked for me. It's difficult when something so personal gets linked into business and becomes your job. You have to really learn to separate things and keep the songwriting pure because there are always pressures on you to deliver commercially. I find that if you try to write something commercial it won't necessarily succeed. I think you have to approach music for the right reason, as an expression. Not something to make you successful as such. The main impulse has to be to express something.

We were lucky because we signed a deal with an independent label and we became successful on the indie label, they were called Infectious Records, and they were always fairly laid back with us really. I think our second album was a big reaction to the success of the first one, which I was quite freaked out by; I couldn't really handle it because I was so young. We made a self-destructive second album that was quite dark. At the time I had writers' block. I felt under so much pressure. I got a lot of attention as a songwriter as well because I was, I guess, prodigious. For my age I'd delivered a lot of good songs and the pressure really crippled me. We made a record that was the complete opposite of what we were known for, and I think that was my way of putting the brakes on, to try and chill things out a bit. But then that album did really badly, we didn't deliver any of the pop tunes we'd been known for. We were really facing extinction as a band! The music industry is so cut-throat, the minute you slip up you're not expected to ever come back from that, especially if you're a young band linked with any kind of scene, and we'd come to prominence during Britpop. At the time our second album was doing badly, many of the other bands who were considered to be Britpop were going through the same thing and getting dropped by their labels. All of a sudden I realised I had to deliver some great songs to stand a chance of keeping the dream alive.

After *Nu-Clear Sounds* I realised that I had to be more disciplined with my songwriting, I had to tap into what I'd done before if we were going to stand a chance of surviving. I went to my parents' house for quite a while, at least six months, nine months; it was the place where I'd written all my best songs before. I hardly went out at all. Joe Strummer was playing in Belfast and he invited me to get up and play 'I Fought The Law' with him. But I didn't even go out to that, I stayed in to write songs. It's kind of stupid, but it's also good. Around that time I wrote 'Shining Light', and the night I wrote 'Shining Light' my girlfriend had said, stay down here in Dublin, but I said, no, I've got to get back up north and get back to work. And I was inspired that night to write 'Shining Light'. Straight away I knew that song was really good. It saved our career, definitely.

You're working on a series of twenty-six singles. That must come with a certain sort of pressure. With albums you have, well, album tracks!

The pressure is sort of the reason we decided to do it. I wanted a massive challenge. With songwriting, the more you practise the easier it is to do. Putting out our last album was very unsatisfactory because albums come and go so quickly. This is a way of each song getting the scrutiny and attention it deserves. For two weeks each song is going to be out there by itself and our fans can digest it.

It took a while before I actually had enough songs that we could start releasing them. I didn't want to fall on my face because I knew people would be quite quick to shoot us down if we didn't produce songs up to a certain quality. They're not all going to be pure mega-hits, of course, but each one can at least be individually interesting. It freed us up to try a lot of new ideas as well because it's a totally different mindset to working on an album. Variety is the key here, which is kind of the opposite of an album where you want to produce a body of work, whereas with this you're looking to shock people as often as possible. We even have a ten-minute instrumental!

In a way, the fact that there are no rules has taken a lot of pressure off. It's given me a new challenge, a new excitement; it's made it fresh for me. To keep challenging yourself is the best way to stay inspired.

chapter eleven:
attack of the Norms

THIS BOOK MAKES TWO general observations about music that might change the way you approach the process of writing songs. The first observation is that every piece of (tonal) music has a tonic note, a tonic chord, a harmonic home. Much of music's interest, tension and power can be attributed to the tension between those notes and chords that are close to home and those that are, to various degrees, far from home.

The second observation is that there are two means by which a composer can play with the expectations of an audience. The composer can establish what is normal for a piece of music in particular by setting, for example, harmonic, rhythmic and melodic precedents as the piece progresses. The composer can then choose the extent to which the piece of music will adhere to these norms and the extent to which it will deviate from them.

Secondly, the composer is able to play with the expectations an audience will bring to a piece of music. Expectations based on genre and the composer's/performer's previous output can be exploited, met and confounded. In other words, there are Norms associated with specific genres that can be played with by the composer, Norms to which a piece of music might adhere and from which it might deviate.

The interplay between norms and Norms is often very complicated, subtle and difficult to describe. It is perhaps the only facet of music that could be described nearly as accurately by a music journalist as it could by a musician. A crude example of interaction between norms and Norms: an imaginary punk rock song deviates from the Norms of punk rock by using the relatively exotic-sounding harmonic minor scale. The song has established the norm of a tonality based upon the harmonic minor scale, and one could argue that the song is all the more unlikely to deviate from this norm because it had to confound the audience's genre-specific expectations to establish it in the first place! On the other hand, one could also argue that the song is more likely to deviate from the norm of a tonality based upon the harmonic minor scale because the song would then be able to relax into the expected tonality of punk rock Norms; that is, a tonality in which major, natural minor or minor pentatonic scales predominate. Neither argument is correct as such; the point is that there would be an utterable interaction between norms and Norms in either case.

Earlier we looked at 'Shining Light', which scarcely deviates – if it deviates at all – from the Norms of the pop-rock genre. It provides us with an archetypal pop song with the expected phrase lengths, structure, changes in harmonic rhythm, instrumentation and so on. It also possesses the qualities needed to corroborate our observation regarding the importance of the tonic note/chord. For example,

'Shining Light' establishes its tonic key emphatically in the opening bars and reaffirms the tonic chord at the beginning of both verse and chorus.

There are countless songs like 'Shining Light', songs that are typical of their genre, songs that have an unambiguous tonic chord. While it is true that such songs constitute the majority of recorded music, there are also thousands of songs in any genre that are more difficult to describe, songs that do not have an obvious tonic chord, for example. Even genres in which we would expect to hear the tonic chord heavily emphasised such as folk and blues have a repertory of songs that are harmonically ambiguous.

'Hey Joe', a song made famous by Jimi Hendrix, is an excellent example of just such a folk/blues song. The sole chord progression from which the song is constructed will almost certainly be known to you as a guitarist. Despite its familiarity, however, it is not an easy progression to understand.

In the majority of cases we would be able to determine the key of a chord progression by cross-referencing its constituent chords with the diatonic chords of probable keys. Cmaj is the first chord in the 'Hey Joe' progression, so we should begin by looking at C major's diatonic chords (see page 186) to see if they match. The chords Dmaj, Amaj and Emaj are not diatonic chords of C major, however. In fact, you will be unable to find a key in which more than three of the song's chords are diatonic. So... what is the tonic key of 'Hey Joe'?

The only way to identify the key of a progression like the one in 'Hey Joe' is to decide which chord sounds like home. In other words, you need to experiment by ending the progression with an extra, final chord of your choice out of the chords that have already appeared in the progression. The task of deciding which of these chords sounds the most final is not at all easy. It might help you to think of the question in these terms; which chord sounds best when played as a concluding chord at the end of the song (progression)?

The harmonic rhythm of 'Hey Joe' gives us valuable information about the song's key. The first four chords of the 'Hey Joe' progression are given a fleeting 2/4 bar each before a change of chord occurs. The last chord, Emaj, is given four bars to itself. Is Emaj the most final-sounding chord for the song?

'Hey Joe' is in the key of E major. This key is difficult to identify because 'Hey Joe' is unusual in its repetition of a single chord progression. A norm is established with the help of this unwavering repetition, that of each chord being the interval of a perfect 5th below (or a perfect 4th above if you prefer) its successor. Cmaj is followed by Gmaj, and G is a perfect 5th above (or a perfect 4th below) C. Gmaj is then followed by Dmaj, and D is a perfect 5th above G.

The progression continues in this fashion until it lands on Emaj, upon which it decides – almost arbitrarily – to 'stick', successfully giving the listener the impression that Emaj was the destination all along. If you did not recognise Emaj as the tonic chord, you may well blame this failure on the music itself for this confidence trick! Had the 'Hey Joe' progression observed the conventions of functional harmony, contextualising the tonic chord by surrounding it with diatonic chords, it is likely that the identity of the tonic chord would have been obvious.

It might come as a surprise to learn that 'Hey Joe' is harmonically unusual. After all, the song is familiar to most guitarists, easy to play and popular among listeners. If you were to sit at the guitar and compose a song with a similar ratio of non-diatonic to diatonic chords the likely outcome would be a song so unusual-sounding that the average listener would find it unpalatable. With this in mind, how does 'Hey Joe' manage to be distinctive and interesting rather than merely... weird-sounding?!

In cases where one aspect of a composition is unusual or complicated it is common to find that other aspects are, conversely, simple. This is particularly true of songs written with the aim of appealing to as many people as possible. The primitive structure of 'Hey Joe' – in which the same chord progression is repeated throughout – acts as a counterweight against the harmonic ambiguity of its singular chord progression. By making all other aspects of a song as simple or as predictable as possible it is possible to mitigate even the strangest harmonic, rhythmic or melodic content.

Simplification is not the only method by which the composer can make unconventional material more palatable to a conventional audience. For example, unconventional or unexpected harmonies are often lubricated by stepwise movements in the outer (typically bass or vocal) parts during chord changes. The presence of a melody or bass line that is either static or moving in increments of a tone or semitone as a chord changes has the effect of making the transition between the chords in question sound more natural, even when these chords are not diatonic.

god only knows

Like 'Hey Joe', The Beach Boys' 'God Only Knows' is a popular, well-known song featuring a recurring, harmonically ambiguous chord progression. Here are the opening 20 bars:

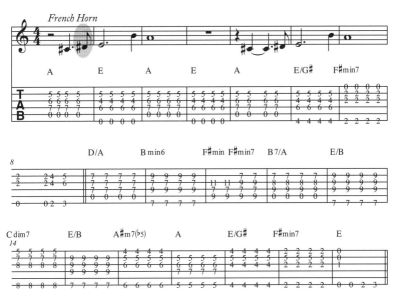

'God Only Knows'

'God Only Knows' begins in the key of E major, which is the song's tonic key. This fact cannot be deduced by looking at the chords alone, however. The chords featured in the first seven bars are Amaj, Emaj and F♯min7, which are all diatonic chords in the key of E major. But they are also diatonic chords in the key of A major, and since the transcribed passage begins on a root-position Amaj chord, A major would seem to be the more likely tonic key.

It is the aim of this book to introduce concepts that have traditionally been the preserve of musicians; specifically, musicians who have been through years of formal musical training. Such musicians would be able to recognise the true tonic key of 'God Only Knows' very quickly by looking not only at the chord names, but also at the stave of conventional notation showing the instrumental melody of the first eight bars. The second note of this melody is D♯, which is a diatonic note in the key of E major. It is not a diatonic note in the key of A major. The significance of this single note – a note played fleetingly by a melodic instrument, a note that is not part of the underlying chord – will only be readily apparent to those readers who are accustomed to reading conventional notation. Because this book is written in such a way that it can be understood by those who do not have a thorough musical training, there will inevitably be blind spots like this one, details whose significance would be obvious to a trained musician and altogether less obvious to the majority of readers.

The D♯ in the instrumental melody in bar 1 gives us important information about the key of 'God Only Knows', but there is a great deal of harmonic ambiguity here. For a start, there is the remarkable absence of a tonic Emaj chord in root position in the opening bars following the introduction, which means the listener is far from certain that the likely tonic key of E major has actually been established. When an E appears in the bass at the start of bar 8 it is as part of a second inversion Amaj chord (Amaj/E) rather than the tonic Emaj.

This uncertainty is compounded by the latter half of bar 8, in which there is a strange-sounding modulation to the key of D major via a third inversion A7 chord (A7/G, the last chord of the bar), which is chord V (chord V7 to be precise) in the key of D major. Play through the introductory bars or listen to the recording to remind yourself just how peculiar this transition into the verse really is!

The fact that the verse begins in a key other than the tonic key is highly unusual. The key of D major, however, is not confirmed with a root-position tonic chord; the D major chord in bar 9 is a second -inversion chord, Dmaj/A. A second-inversion chord is significantly weaker than a root-position chord in this context, and second-inversion chords are used relatively rarely in the conventional genres of recorded music such as pop, rock, soul and so on. It is a measure of this song's cultivation of harmonic uncertainty that a second-inversion chord in a key other than the tonic is the opening chord of the verse and the chord over which the voice first enters.

It is not long before the verse moves towards the key of E major. It re-establishes the tonic key, however, only in a very weak sense; and let's not forget that the key of E major was never firmly established to begin with. The change of key happens in bars 12 and 13, in which a third inversion B7 chord (B7/A) resolves to a second inversion Emaj chord (Emaj/B) – chord V7 to chord I in the key of E major. Eagle-eyed readers will notice that this modulation mirrors the last; A7/G to Dmaj/A and B7/A to Emaj/B establish their respective keys with the same harmonic relationship.

Once again, the listener is not able to feel secure about the song's harmonic orientation. No sooner have we arrived at the tonic chord of the tonic key – albeit in its second inversion – than we are hit with a non-diatonic chord, a Cdim7 in bar 14. Similarly, the Emaj/B in bar 15 is followed by yet another non-diatonic chord, A♯min7♭5, in bar 16. So what's going on?

These non-diatonic chords can be understood as having a relationship with the tonic key. Once again, however, the knowledge required to understand these chords in such a manner is not to be found within these pages. A musicologist or classically trained musician, for example, might see the Cdim7 as actually being a B♯dim7 (don't ask...) that would be understood best in relation to the relative minor key of C♯ minor, while the A♯min7♭5 could be understood in relation to chord V (Bmaj) in the tonic key. These subtleties are not important right now, though.

As a songwriter, it is most important that you recognise two qualities of bars 13–16:

> *1. Non-diatonic chords alternate with diatonic chords. Because the tonic key of E major has not yet been firmly established, these non-diatonic chords undermine whatever little sense the listener may have had of the tonic key's identity.*

> *2. The bass line moves in increments of no more than a tone in bars 12–20. The stepwise motion of the bass line in bars 13–16 (B, C, B, A♯) smoothes the transition between distantly related chords and mitigates the degree to which these chord changes might startle the listener.*

The four-bar chorus follows, repeating the chords of bars 4–8 of the introduction with one major difference; the second inversion Amaj chord in bar 8 is replaced by – at last! – the tonic chord of Emaj in root position in bar 20.

attack of the Norms II: the reckoning

It should be obvious that the composers of 'God Only Knows' and 'Hey Joe' took very different routes to their respective root-position Emaj chords. 'God Only Knows' is sophisticated in its ambiguity in that it flirts with the tonic key, but never settles down. Even the final Emaj chord of the progression is quickly undermined by the non-diatonic G♮ in the bass that follows.

'Hey Joe' is altogether less sophisticated. It has the demeanour of a song written at the guitar where the guitarist's fingers have controlled the process of composition reflexively, adopting familiar hand positions until a successful combination of chords has emerged. 'Hey Joe' is not 'composed' in the way 'God Only Knows' is 'composed'; its harmonies, melodies and structure have not been evaluated, re-evaluated and revised.

These two distinct approaches to songwriting are representative of two virtues that have competed for audiences' appreciation since the 1960s: authenticity and ingenuity. Though rarely spoken about in such explicit terms, nothing has distinguished the aesthetic of one listener from another more than a preference for one of these qualities over its competitor. It is one of authenticity's requirements that a composition should not seem to have been carefully thought about and refined by the composer, that it should not betray the influence of a formal musical training in particular. Above all, a composition must not be susceptible to the charge of seeming contrived.

It is easy enough to compile a list of acts whose music has been criticised for being too contrived: The Beach Boys, David Bowie, Queen, Billy Joel, ELO, The Smiths, The Divine Comedy, Elliott Smith, Fiona Apple, The Strokes, Muse and so on. These acts are often calculating and clever in their songwriting, particularly in their use of harmony and the way they structure their songs. They have self-consciously forsaken authenticity to some degree in that they pay little homage to the Norms of pop's progenitorial genres, folk and blues. Many listeners regard relatively convoluted music as being less 'real' than stripped-down music by, for example, Neil Young, The Sex Pistols or The White Stripes, and certainly less 'real' than the music of Robert Johnson or Blind Lemon Jefferson.

As a guitar-playing songwriter, your instrument provides you with a direct line to the early folk and blues musicians who were the founding fathers of pop music in all its guises. Most recorded music today is calculated to appeal to those who value authenticity and those who value ingenuity alike; of course, the result is often unconvincing on both fronts as a quick listen to the latest mainstream pop singles will tell you. However, while authenticity is a highly marketable quality that can give an artist the all-important appearance of credibility, ingenuity is a harder sell, and it would be nothing short of uncanny to see a song of 'God Only Knows" sophistication in the charts today. With this in mind, and considering that you play the instrument of authenticity, you may be asking yourself what you could possibly gain by endeavouring to understand a difficult, 'contrived' song like 'God Only Knows'. By sticking to diatonic harmony and guitaristic progressions and riffs in your own songwriting, are you not giving yourself the best chance of commercial success, success that might be prohibited by a more sophisticated approach to composition or the acquisition of a musical education?

This is a common concern among songwriters and musicians who belong to a tradition of folk music, including bastardised forms of folk music such as mainstream rock, pop or modern R n B. Unlike the traditions of classical music and jazz, in which a formal musical education is normal and technique – both instrumental and compositional – is taught and practised with stilted rigour, folk music is associated with the hardship, slavery and victimisation of many of its greatest exponents. Songwriters and musicians who see themselves as belonging to this tradition and its sub-genres are suspicious of any association with formal education, partly because the influence of formal education might corrupt the genre by undermining its uneducated origins, and partly because education has always been an instrument of social stratification and oppression. The modern blues guitarist worries that by refining his technique he risks losing his 'feel'. The modern songwriter worries that his education will show through and unplug his music from its uneducated and oppressed power source, placing his music on the side of the oppressors by association. This is a simplification, of course. But these are ideas made more and more simplistic by successive generations of the music industry's appointed arbiters of musical taste, be they record company executives, music journalists or musicians. It is stylish to say that the music industry has always been as cynical as it is today, and while this often-heard statement might be true, it overlooks an important distinction between authenticity as it was valued by audiences from the 1950s to the early 70s and authenticity as it exists in the minds of audiences and musicians today. The pursuit of credibility undertaken by British musicians in the 1960s, for example, took the form of an assimilation and reinvention of American blues and folk music, and while one could argue that this pursuit was often redolent of opportunism, there can be no question that it was prefigured by genuine excitement about American folk and blues among musicians and audiences. By contrast, there is more than a hint of manufactured excitement about the origins of the British punk movement of the late 70s; the new sort of authenticity to which it aspired required salesmanship from the very beginning in a way that the blues-oriented authenticity pursued by bands from the 60s did not.

The sort of authenticity promoted by the music industry in the twenty-first century so far has been so feeble-minded as to be almost incomprehensible. Record companies like to think they can keep the idea of authenticity alive and manufacture some backwards-looking excitement by dressing a female artist as Dusty Springfield and bringing in a trombonist, or by telling a rock band to sound and look like Led Zeppelin circa 1969. The problem is that authenticity in this sense is not really the source of energy it pretends to be. It is disconnected from the forces that made the idea of authenticity important in the first place, and not even the music of a self-determined artist such as Jack White (who certainly makes the best of a bad situation) can dispel the unspoken suspicion among listeners that the modern-day selling points of realness and authenticity are nothing more than exactly that; selling points. In this regard, the corporate model – whereby a commercially successful phenomenon must be turned into a formula for the purpose of endless reconstitution – has injured the culture of recorded music by selling and re-selling this now-empty idea of authenticity with such vigour that the emergence of musical trends with any potency or originality has been inhibited to the point of their extinction.

The question of whether a songwriter can harm his chances of success merely by having educated himself is as spurious as the hollowed-out idea of authenticity from which it stems. A folk musician is no more likely to lose his mojo by acquiring an understanding of functional harmony than Stravinsky would be to forget his classical training after spending a day with Muddy Waters. If a songwriter were to make it his mission to stick to the most predictable, root position, rhythmically square chord progressions possible, even these compositions would benefit from his ability to understand compositions of 'God Only Knows'' complexity.

It goes without saying that the question of precisely how a songwriter will utilise an understanding of the mechanics of songwriting can only be answered by the songwriter himself. This book is not intended to invoke a radical change of artistic direction in its readership. It is intended to empower the reader by providing a view of mechanisms that might otherwise have remained hidden. However, it is also hoped that a consideration of other, less mechanical issues will arise from these modest revelations, and this consideration may alter something fundamental in your approach to songwriting.

appendix a:
note names

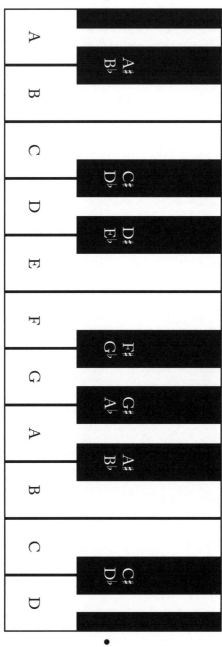

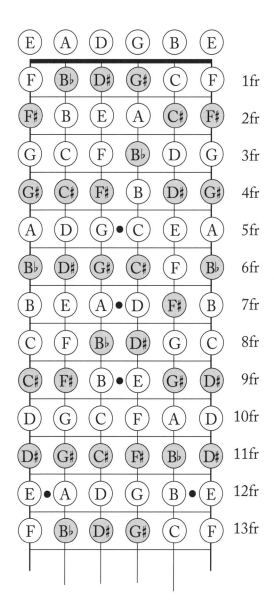

appendix b:
diatonic chords in guitaristic keys

C major

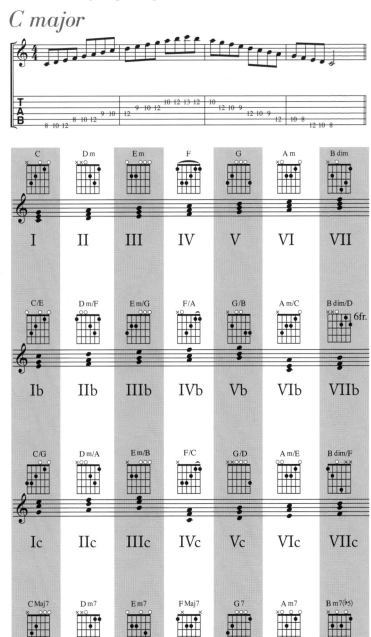

D major

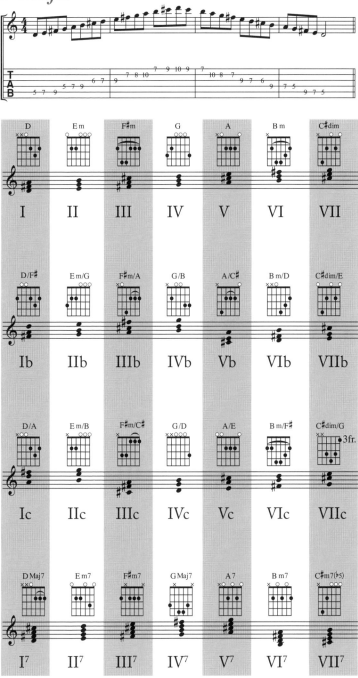

E major

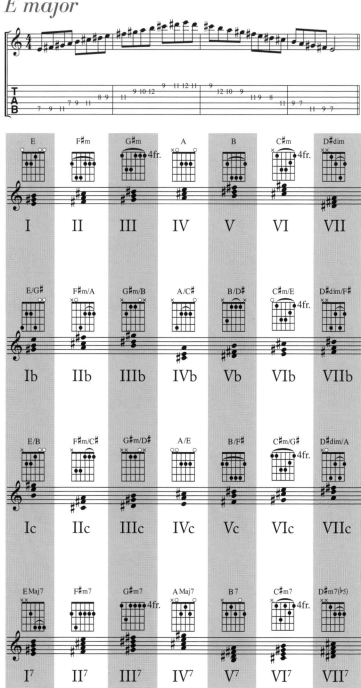

F major

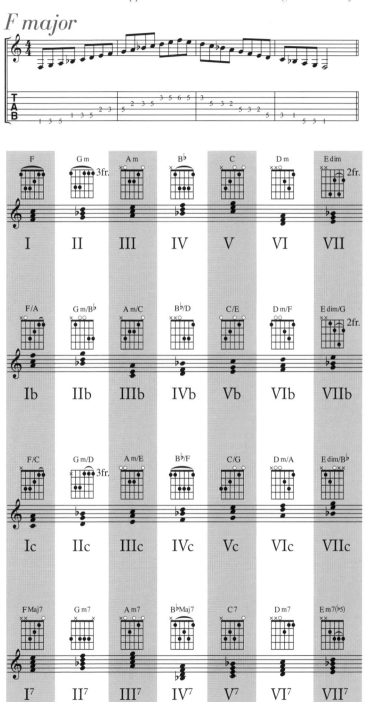

G major

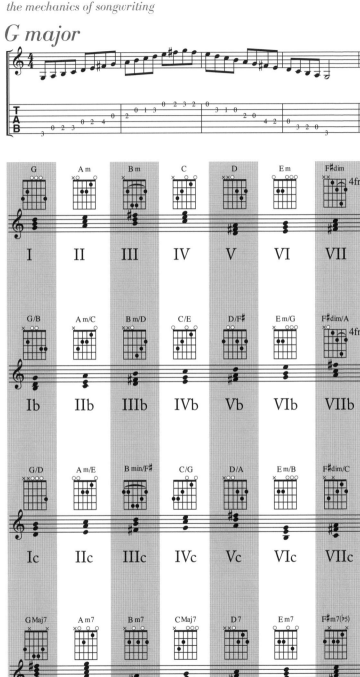

A major

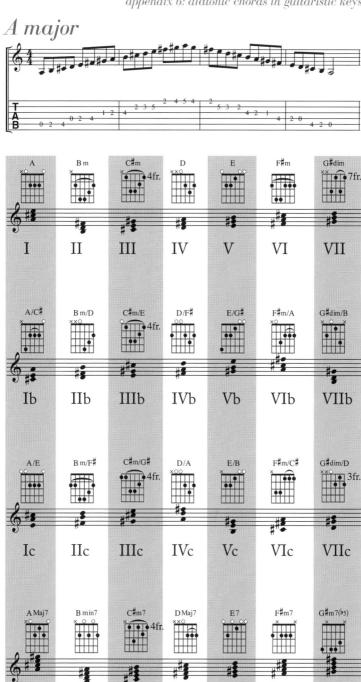

A minor

Natural · Harmonic

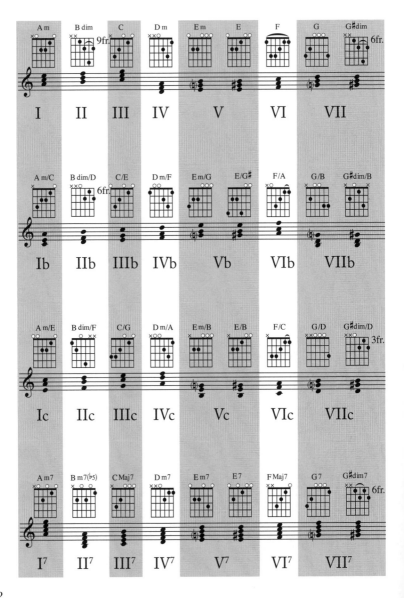

B minor

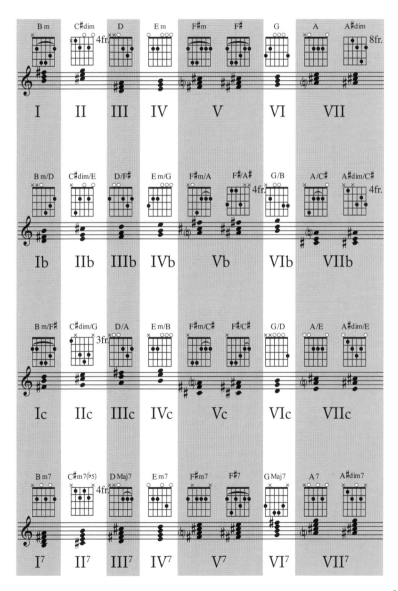

C# minor

Natural   **Harmonic**

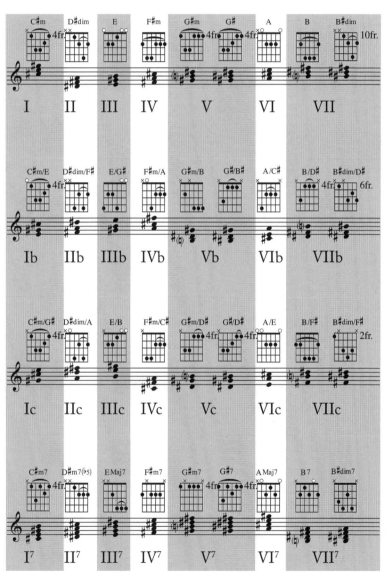

D minor

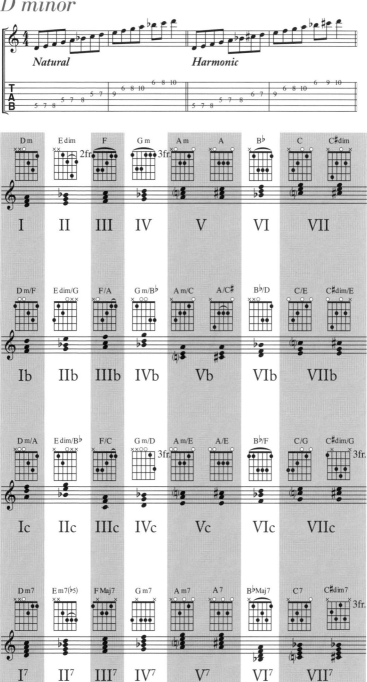

E minor

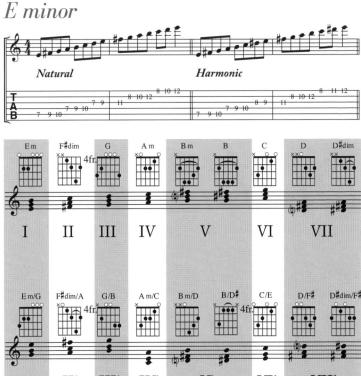

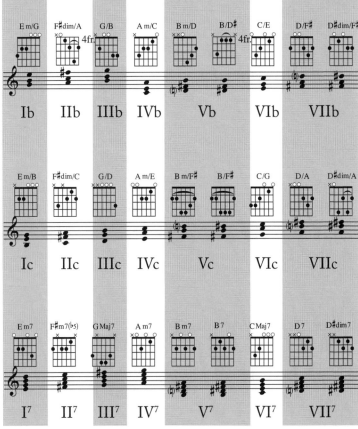

F# minor

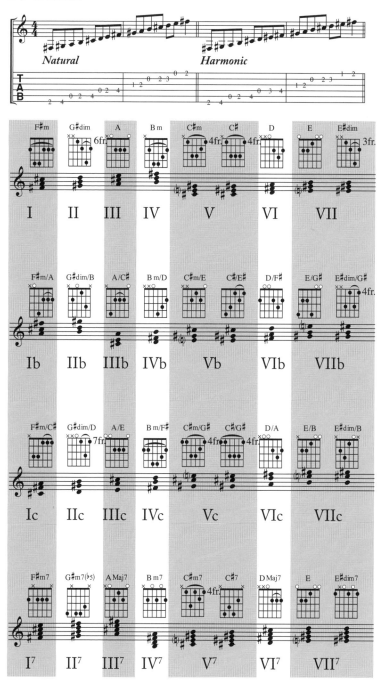

glossary

♯ **or sharp** Modifies a pitch so that it is one semitone higher (sharper) than it would be normally.

♭ **or flat** Modifies a pitch so that it is one semitone lower (flatter) than it would be normally.

♮ **or natural** Shows that a pitch is not or is no longer sharp or flat.

Arpeggio A term for a broken chord, a chord that is broken up so that each of its notes is played individually, one after another.

Blue note A specific non-diatonic note in a pentatonic context; a note either a major 3rd or an augmented 4th above the first note of the relevant pentatonic scale.

Bridge A distinct section of a song linking verse and chorus.

Cadence A succession of at least two chords that conclude a musical phrase. A perfect cadence - which concludes the vast majority of pieces written in the western world during the eighteenth and nineteenth centuries - consists of chord V followed by chord I.

Chord progression A series of chords.

Chromatic Of or reminiscent of a chromatic scale.

Coda See outro.

Consonance A chord or interval that is commonly regarded as sounding pleasant or 'stable'. The harmonic intervals of a perfect 5th and a major 3rd are generally regarded as consonant. *See also dissonance.*

Counterpoint The relationship between two (or more) instrumental parts or voices that move independently of one another.

Chorus The recurring section of a song that usually appears at least twice in an unaltered form, with the same music and lyrics each time.

Diatonic Notes that belong to a given major or minor scale, or anything that consists of these notes. In the context of a discussion of a piece of music and its key, 'diatonic' refers to notes that belong to the scale of the same name as the key in question.

Dissonance A chord or interval that is commonly regarded as sounding unpleasant or 'unstable'. The harmonic intervals of a minor 2nd and a major 7th are generally regarded as dissonant. *See also consonance.*

Dominant The fifth degree of a major or minor scale and the chord thereof.

Harmonic rhythm The rate at which chords change.

Intro A distinct section of a song that precedes the first appearance of verse and chorus.

Inversion Describes a chord in relation to its lowest-pitched note.

Key Broadly, key describes the expected harmonic vocabulary of a piece or passage of music.

Key signature The sharps or flats at the beginning of a stave of conventionally notated music that denote key.

Leading note The seventh degree of a major scale; also, the seventh degree of a harmonic minor scale. The seventh degree of a natural minor scale should be referred to as the subtonic rather than the leading note.

Legato An Italian term describing music that is played (or is to be played) smoothly, without an audible gap between successive notes.

Line A term appropriated in this book to describe the directionality of musical material.

Major and minor The two most important scales in western music, each consisting of seven notes. The principal difference between major and minor scales is the interval between the tonic note and the third note of the scale. These notes are separated by four semitones in the case of major scales and three semitones in the case of minor scales. Keys, intervals and chords can also be described as major or minor.

Melisma In a vocal part, melisma occurs when a single syllable of a lyric is carried by several notes in succession.

Middle C The C that is located closest to the centre of an eighty-eight-key piano keyboard; a C of that pitch.

Middle-eight A section of new material introduced relatively late in a song, typically lasting eight bars.

Modulation Movement from one key to another within a piece of music.

Motif A recurring musical idea.

Norms Within the confines of this book, the word 'norms' refers specifically to precedents established by a particular piece of music that are reinforced or confounded as the piece progresses. The word 'Norms' refers to precedents established by musical style and genre, which a piece of music might follow or from which it might deviate.

Octave The interval consisting of twelve semitones in either direction between a given note and the two nearest pitches of the same name. The G on the fifth fret of the D string is an octave lower than the G on the third fret of the high (thin) E string, while it is an octave higher than the G on the third fret of the low (thick) E string. The G on the third fret of the high E string is two octaves higher than the G on the third fret of the low E string.

Outro A distinct section of music that concludes a song.

Pentatonic A scale consisting of five notes.

Phrase There is no satisfactory way of defining the musical phrase. If you feel that a unit of musical material lasting between four and eight bars has integrity - a beginning and an end - then you might describe it as a phrase.

Pivot chord A chord common to both keys involved in a modulation.

Relative major/minor A key or scale that shares a key signature with its minor/major equivalent.

Riff A short, catchy instrumental motif usually played in the guitar's lower register.

Root The note after which a chord is named; the note D in the chord of D minor, for example.

Suspension The dissonance that arises from the carrying over of a note from one chord into the chord that follows.

Syllabic A vocal part is syllabic when each syllable of the lyrics is sung by an individual note.

Time signature A specification of the number of (equal) beats in each bar. 4/4 is the most common time signature, which specifies four beats in each bar.

Tonic The first degree of a scale and the note or chord that is the harmonic centre or 'home' of a key.

Transpose To move a note or a group of notes to a new pitch. You could transpose an existing piece of music to a new key, for example.

Triad A three-note chord consisting of root, third and fifth.

Verse A recurring section of a song characterised by the combination of the same music and different lyrics in each recurrence.

index

index of exercises

acknowledgements

Siduri Books would like to thank the following contributors:

Tim Wheeler, Eric Bazilian and Stephin Merritt for sharing their insights into the art of songwriting and taking the requests of a small publisher seriously.

Laura Howell, comic artist extraordinaire, for her wonderful and humorous illustrations.

Siduri Books would also like to thank the following for allowing us to reproduce extracts from songs:

Sunshine Of Your Love
Words & Music by Jack Bruce, Pete Brown & Eric Clapton
© Copyright 1967 & 1996 Warner/Chappell Music Limited (66.66%)/
Eric Clapton (33.34%).
All Rights Reserved. International Copyright Secured.
Used by permission of Music Sales Limited.

God Only Knows
Words & Music by Brian Douglas Wilson & Tony Asher
© Copyright Universal Music Publ. Ltd.
All Rights Reserved. International Copyright Secured.
Used by permission of Music Sales Limited.

Shining Light
Words & Music by Tim Wheeler
© Copyright 2001 Universal/Island Music Limited.
All Rights Reserved. International Copyright Secured.
Used by permission of Music Sales Limited.

Time Is Running Out
Words and Music by Matthew Bellamy
© 2003 Hewrate Ltd
Warner/Chappell Music Publishing Ltd, London W6 8BS
Reproduced by permission of Faber Music Ltd
All Rights Reserved.

The author would like to thank:

GM and DM, for the author's continuity.